*~ All Time ~*

# FAMILY FAVORITES™

# GRANDMA'S OLD-FASHIONED COOKIES

PUBLICATIONS INTERNATIONAL, LTD.

**Pictured on the front cover:** Peanut Butter Sensations *(page 6),* Original Nestlé® Toll House® Chocolate Chip Cookies *(page 42),* Luscious Lemon Bars *(page 70),* Caramel-Layered Brownies *(page 80)* and Linzer Sandwich Cookies *(page 122).*

**Pictured on the back cover** *(top to bottom):* Peachy Oatmeal Bars *(page 60)* and Streusel Strawberry Bars *(page 60).*

# — Contents —

# COOKIE-JAR FAVORITES

## CHOCOLATE-DIPPED ALMOND HORNS

1½ **cups powdered sugar**
1 **cup butter or margarine, softened**
2 **egg yolks**
1½ **teaspoons vanilla**
2 **cups all-purpose flour**
½ **cup ground almonds**
1 **teaspoon cream of tartar**
1 **teaspoon baking soda**
1 **cup semisweet chocolate chips, melted**
**Powdered sugar**

Preheat oven to 325°F. In large bowl, combine powdered sugar and butter. Beat at medium speed until creamy. Add egg yolks and vanilla; continue beating until well blended. Reduce speed to low. Add flour, almonds, cream of tartar and baking soda. Continue beating until well mixed. Shape into 1-inch balls. Roll balls into 2-inch ropes; shape into crescents. Place 2 inches apart on cookie sheets. Flatten slightly with bottom of glass covered in waxed paper. Bake for 8 to 10 minutes or until set. (Cookies do not brown.) Cool completely. Dip half of each cookie into chocolate; sprinkle remaining half with powdered sugar. Refrigerate until set.

*Makes about 3 dozen cookies*

## OATMEAL APPLE COOKIES

¾ **CRISCO® Stick or ¾ cup CRISCO®
All-Vegetable Shortening**
1¼ **cups firmly packed brown sugar**
1 **egg**
¼ **cup milk**
1½ **teaspoons vanilla**
1 **cup all-purpose flour**
1¼ **teaspoons ground cinnamon**
½ **teaspoon salt**
¼ **teaspoon baking soda**
¼ **teaspoon ground nutmeg**
3 **cups quick oats (not instant or
old-fashioned)**
1 **cup peeled, diced apples**
¾ **cup raisins (optional)**
¾ **cup coarsely chopped walnuts (optional)**

**1.** Preheat oven to 375°F. Grease cookie sheet with shortening.

**2.** Combine shortening, sugar, egg, milk and vanilla in large bowl. Beat at medium speed of electric mixer until well blended.

**3.** Combine flour, cinnamon, salt, baking soda and nutmeg in small bowl. Mix into creamed mixture at low speed until just blended. Stir in, one at a time, oats, apples, raisins and nuts with spoon.

**4.** Drop rounded tablespoonfuls of dough 2 inches apart onto cookie sheet.

**5.** Bake at 375°F for 13 minutes or until set. Cool 2 minutes on cookie sheet. Remove to wire rack. Cool completely.      *Makes about 2½ dozen cookies*

## PEANUT BUTTER SENSATIONS

½ **CRISCO® Stick or ½ cup CRISCO®
All-Vegetable Shortening**
1 **cup JIF® Creamy Peanut Butter**
¾ **cup granulated sugar**
½ **cup firmly packed brown sugar**
1 **tablespoon milk**
1 **teaspoon vanilla**
1 **egg**
1¼ **cups all-purpose flour**
¾ **teaspoon baking soda**
½ **teaspoon baking powder**
¼ **teaspoon salt**

**1.** Preheat oven to 375°F.

**2.** Combine shortening, peanut butter, granulated sugar, brown sugar, milk and vanilla in large bowl. Beat at medium speed of electric mixer until well blended. Beat in egg.

**3.** Combine flour, baking soda, baking powder and salt in small bowl. Mix into creamed mixture at low speed until just blended. Drop rounded tablespoonfuls of dough 2 inches apart onto ungreased cookie sheet. Make crisscross pattern on dough with floured fork.

**4.** Bake at 375°F for 8 to 10 minutes. Cool 2 minutes on cookie sheet. Remove to wire rack. Cool completely.      *Makes about 2 dozen cookies*

*Oatmeal Apple Cookies*

COOKIE-JAR FAVORITES

# CHOCOLATE SUGAR COOKIES

**3 squares BAKER'S® Unsweetened Chocolate**
**1 cup (2 sticks) margarine or butter**
**1 cup sugar**
**1 egg**
**1 teaspoon vanilla**
**2 cups all-purpose flour**
**1 teaspoon baking soda**
**¼ teaspoon salt**
**Additional sugar**

MICROWAVE chocolate and margarine in large microwavable bowl on HIGH 2 minutes or until margarine is melted. **Stir until chocolate is completely melted.**

STIR 1 cup sugar into melted chocolate mixture until well blended. Stir in egg and vanilla until completely mixed. Mix in flour, baking soda and salt. Refrigerate 30 minutes.

HEAT oven to 375°F. Shape dough into 1-inch balls; roll in additional sugar. Place on ungreased cookie sheets. (If a flatter, crisper cookie is desired, flatten ball with bottom of drinking glass.)

BAKE for 8 to 10 minutes or until set. Remove from cookie sheets to cool on wire racks.
*Makes about 3½ dozen cookies*

**Prep Time:** 15 minutes
**Chill Time:** 30 minutes
**Baking Time:** 8 to 10 minutes

**JAM-FILLED CHOCOLATE SUGAR COOKIES: PREPARE** Chocolate Sugar Cookie dough as directed. Roll in finely chopped nuts in place of sugar. Make indentation in each ball; fill center with your favorite jam. Bake as directed.

**CHOCOLATE-CARAMEL SUGAR COOKIES: PREPARE** Chocolate Sugar Cookie dough as directed. Roll in finely chopped nuts in place of sugar. Make indentation in each ball; bake as directed. Microwave 1 package (14 ounces) KRAFT® Caramels with 2 tablespoons milk in microwavable bowl on HIGH 3 minutes or until melted, stirring after 2 minutes. Fill centers of cookies with caramel mixture. Drizzle with melted BAKER'S® Semi-Sweet Chocolate.

*Top to bottom: Chocolate Sugar Cookies, Jam-Filled Chocolate Sugar Cookies, Chocolate-Caramel Sugar Cookies*

## JAM-UP OATMEAL COOKIES

**1 CRISCO® Stick or 1 cup CRISCO®
   All-Vegetable Shortening
1½ cups firmly packed brown sugar
2 eggs
2 teaspoons almond extract
2 cups all-purpose flour
1 teaspoon baking powder
1 teaspoon salt
½ teaspoon baking soda
2½ cups quick oats (not instant or
   old-fashioned), uncooked
1 cup finely chopped pecans
1 jar (12 ounces) strawberry jam
   Sugar for sprinkling**

**1.** Combine shortening and brown sugar in large bowl. Beat at medium speed of electric mixer until well blended. Beat in eggs and almond extract.

**2.** Combine flour, baking powder, salt and baking soda in small bowl. Mix into creamed mixture at low speed until just blended. Stir in oats and chopped nuts with spoon. Cover and refrigerate at least 1 hour.

**3.** Preheat oven to 350°F. Grease cookie sheet with shortening. Roll out dough, half at a time, to about ¼-inch thickness on floured surface. Cut out with 2½-inch round cookie cutter. Place 1 teaspoonful of jam in center of half of the rounds. Top with remaining rounds. Press edges to seal. Prick centers; sprinkle with sugar. Place 1 inch apart on cookie sheet.

**4.** Bake 12 to 15 minutes or until lightly browned. Cool 2 minutes on cookie sheet. Remove to wire rack. Cool completely.

*Makes about 2 dozen cookies*

## PEANUT BUTTER JEWELS

**1 package DUNCAN HINES® Peanut Butter
   Cookie Mix
1 egg
¼ cup CRISCO® Oil
1 tablespoon water
⅓ cup sugar
⅓ cup cocktail peanuts, finely chopped
   Strawberry jam
   Apricot preserves**

**1.** Preheat oven to 375°F.

**2.** Combine cookie mix, peanut butter flavor packet from Mix, egg, oil and water in large bowl. Stir until thoroughly blended. Shape dough into 48 (1-inch) balls. Roll half the balls in sugar and half in chopped peanuts. Place 2 inches apart on ungreased cookie sheets. Make indentation in center of each ball with finger or handle end of wooden spoon. Fill with ¼ teaspoon strawberry jam or apricot preserves. Bake at 375°F for 8 to 10 minutes or until light golden brown. Cool 1 minute on cookie sheets. Remove to wire racks. Cool completely. Store in airtight containers.

*Makes 4 dozen cookies*

**TIP:** For a delicious flavor variation, try seedless red raspberry or blackberry jam.

*Jam-Up Oatmeal Cookies*

COOKIE-JAR FAVORITES

## COCOA SNICKERDOODLES

1 cup butter or margarine, softened
¾ cup firmly packed brown sugar
¾ cup plus 2 tablespoons granulated sugar, divided
2 eggs
2 cups uncooked rolled oats
1½ cups all-purpose flour
¼ cup plus 2 tablespoons unsweetened cocoa powder, divided
1 teaspoon baking soda
2 tablespoons ground cinnamon

Preheat oven to 375°F. Lightly grease cookie sheets or line with parchment paper. Beat butter, brown sugar and ¾ cup granulated sugar in large bowl until light and fluffy. Add eggs; mix well. Combine oats, flour, ¼ cup cocoa and baking soda in medium bowl. Stir into butter mixture until blended. Mix remaining 2 tablespoons granulated sugar, cinnamon and remaining 2 tablespoons cocoa in small bowl. Drop dough by rounded teaspoonfuls into cinnamon mixture; toss to coat. Place 2 inches apart on prepared cookie sheets. Bake 8 to 10 minutes or until firm in center. *Do not overbake.* Remove to wire racks to cool.

*Makes about 4½ dozen cookies*

## SPICY PUMPKIN COOKIES

2 CRISCO® Sticks or 2 cups CRISCO® All-Vegetable Shortening
2 cups sugar
1 can (16 ounces) solid pack pumpkin
2 eggs
2 teaspoons vanilla
4 cups all-purpose flour
2 teaspoons baking powder
2 teaspoons ground cinnamon
1 teaspoon salt
1 teaspoon baking soda
1 teaspoon ground nutmeg
½ teaspoon ground allspice
2 cups raisins
1 cup chopped nuts

**1.** Preheat oven to 350°F.

**2.** Combine shortening, sugar, pumpkin, eggs and vanilla in large bowl; beat well.

**3.** Combine flour, baking powder, cinnamon, salt, baking soda, nutmeg and allspice in medium bowl. Add to pumpkin mixture; mix well. Stir in raisins and nuts. Drop rounded teaspoonfuls of dough, 2 inches apart, onto greased cookie sheet.

**4.** Bake at 350°F for 12 to 15 minutes. Cool on wire rack. If desired, frost with vanilla frosting.

*Makes about 7 dozen cookies*

*Chocolate-Peanut Cookies (page 36),*
*Cocoa Snickerdoodles*

# RASPBERRY ALMOND SANDWICH COOKIES

**1 package DUNCAN HINES® Golden Sugar Cookie Mix**
**1 egg**
**¼ cup CRISCO® Oil**
**1 tablespoon water**
**¾ teaspoon almond extract**
**1⅓ cups sliced natural almonds, broken Seedless red raspberry jam**

**1.** Preheat oven to 375°F.

**2.** Combine cookie mix, egg, oil, water and almond extract in large bowl. Stir until thoroughly blended. Drop half the dough by level measuring teaspoons 2 inches apart onto ungreased cookie sheets. (It is a small amount of dough but will spread during baking to 1½ to 1¾ inches.)

**3.** Place almonds on waxed paper. Drop other half of dough by level measuring teaspoons onto nuts. Place almond side up 2 inches apart on cookie sheets.

**4.** Bake both plain and almond cookies at 375°F for 6 minutes or until set but not browned. Cool 1 minute on cookie sheets. Remove to wire racks. Cool completely.

**5.** Spread bottoms of plain cookies with jam; top with almond cookies. Press together to make sandwiches. Store in airtight containers.

*Makes 6 dozen sandwich cookies*

# OLD-FASHIONED OATMEAL COOKIES

**¾ CRISCO® Stick or ¾ cup CRISCO® All-Vegetable Shortening**
**1¼ cups firmly packed brown sugar**
**1 egg**
**⅓ cup milk**
**1½ teaspoons vanilla**
**1 cup all-purpose flour**
**½ teaspoon baking soda**
**½ teaspoon salt**
**¼ teaspoon ground cinnamon**
**3 cups quick oats (not instant or old-fashioned)**
**1 cup raisins**
**1 cup coarsely chopped walnuts**

**1.** Preheat oven to 375°F. Grease cookie sheet.

**2.** Combine shortening, sugar, egg, milk and vanilla in large bowl. Beat at medium speed of electric mixer until well blended.

**3.** Combine flour, baking soda, salt and cinnamon in small bowl. Mix into creamed mixture at low speed until just blended. Stir in oats, raisins and nuts with spoon.

**4.** Drop rounded tablespoonfuls of dough 2 inches apart onto cookie sheet.

**5.** Bake at 375°F for 10 to 12 minutes or until lightly browned. Cool 2 minutes on cookie sheet. Remove to wire rack. Cool completely.

*Makes about 2½ dozen cookies*

*Raspberry Almond Sandwich Cookies*

## MOM'S BEST OATMEAL COOKIES

**1 CRISCO® Stick or 1 cup CRISCO®**
 **All-Vegetable Shortening**
**1½ cups firmly packed brown sugar**
 **2 eggs**
 **2 teaspoons vanilla**
**1½ cups all-purpose flour**
 **1 teaspoon salt**
 **1 teaspoon baking powder**
 **1 teaspoon ground cinnamon**
 **¼ teaspoon baking soda**
 **2 cups quick oats (not instant or**
  **old-fashioned)**
 **1 cup chopped pecans**
 **⅔ cup sesame seeds**
 **⅔ cup flaked coconut**

**1.** Preheat oven to 350°F.

**2.** Combine shortening and sugar in large bowl. Beat at medium speed of electric mixer until well blended. Beat in eggs and vanilla.

**3.** Combine flour, salt, baking powder, cinnamon and baking soda in small bowl. Mix into creamed mixture at low speed until blended. Stir in, one at a time, oats, nuts, sesame seeds and coconut with spoon. Drop rounded tablespoonfuls of dough 2 inches apart onto ungreased cookie sheet.

**4.** Bake at 350°F for 10 minutes or until lightly browned. Remove immediately to wire rack. Cool completely. *Makes about 6 dozen cookies*

## GINGER SNAP OATS

**¾ CRISCO® Stick or ¾ cup CRISCO®**
 **All-Vegetable Shortening**
 **1 cup firmly packed brown sugar**
 **½ cup granulated sugar**
 **½ cup molasses**
 **2 teaspoons vinegar**
 **2 eggs**
**1¼ cups all-purpose flour**
 **1 tablespoon ground ginger**
**1½ teaspoons baking soda**
 **½ teaspoon ground cinnamon**
 **¼ teaspoon ground cloves**
**2¾ cups quick oats (not instant or**
  **old-fashioned)**
**1½ cups raisins**

**1.** Preheat oven to 350°F. Grease cookie sheet with shortening.

**2.** Combine shortening, brown sugar, granulated sugar, molasses, vinegar and eggs in large bowl. Beat at medium speed of electric mixer until well blended.

**3.** Combine flour, ginger, baking soda, cinnamon and cloves in small bowl. Mix into creamed mixture at low speed until blended. Stir in oats and raisins. Drop rounded teaspoonfuls of dough 2 inches apart onto cookie sheet.

**4.** Bake at 350°F for 11 to 14 minutes. Cool 2 minutes on cookie sheet. Remove to wire rack. Cool completely. *Makes about 5 dozen cookies*

*Top to bottom: Ginger Snap Oats, Mom's Best Oatmeal Cookies*

## VIENNESE HAZELNUT BUTTER THINS

**1 cup hazelnuts**
**1¼ cups powdered sugar**
**1 cup butter, softened**
**1 large egg**
**1 teaspoon vanilla**
**1¼ cups all-purpose flour**
**¼ teaspoon salt**
**1 cup semisweet chocolate chips**

**1.** Preheat oven to 350°F. Spread hazelnuts in single layer on baking sheet. Bake 10 to 12 minutes or until toasted and skins begin to flake off; let cool slightly. Wrap nuts in heavy kitchen towel; rub to remove as much of the skins as possible. Process nuts in food processor until nuts are ground, but not pasty.

**2.** Beat powdered sugar and butter in medium bowl with electric mixer at medium speed until light and fluffy. Beat in egg and vanilla. Gradually add flour and salt. Beat in nuts at low speed.

**3.** Place dough on sheet of waxed paper. Roll back and forth to form a log 12 inches long and 2½ inches wide. Wrap in plastic wrap and refrigerate until firm, 2 hours or up to 48 hours.

**4.** Preheat oven to 350°F. Cut dough with knife crosswise into ¼-inch-thick slices. Place cookies 2 inches apart on *ungreased* cookie sheets.

**5.** Bake 10 to 12 minutes or until edges are very lightly browned. Let cookies stand on cookie sheets 1 minute. Remove cookies with spatula to wire racks; cool completely.

**6.** Melt chocolate chips in 2-cup glass measure in microwave at HIGH 2½ to 3 minutes, stirring once. Dip each cookie into chocolate, coating half way up sides. Let excess chocolate drip back into cup. Transfer cookies to waxed paper; let stand at room temperature 1 hour or until set. Store tightly covered between sheets of waxed paper at room temperature or freeze up to 3 months.

*Makes about 3 dozen cookies*

## RAISIN SPICE DROPS

**¾ cup (1½ sticks) margarine, softened**
**⅔ cup firmly packed brown sugar**
**⅔ cup granulated sugar**
**2 eggs**
**1 teaspoon vanilla**
**2½ cups QUAKER® Oats (quick or old-fashioned, uncooked)**
**1¼ cups all-purpose flour**
**1 teaspoon ground cinnamon**
**½ teaspoon baking soda**
**½ teaspoon salt (optional)**
**¼ teaspoon ground nutmeg**
**⅔ cup raisins**
**½ cup chopped nuts**

Preheat oven to 350°F. In large bowl, beat margarine and sugars until fluffy. Blend in eggs and vanilla. Add remaining ingredients; mix well. Drop dough by rounded teaspoonfuls onto ungreased cookie sheet. Bake 8 to 10 minutes or until light golden brown. Cool on wire rack. Store tightly covered.     *Makes about 4½ dozen cookies*

*Viennese Hazelnut Butter Thins*

## SWISS MOCHA TREATS

**2 ounces imported Swiss bittersweet
   chocolate candy bar, broken**
**½ cup plus 2 tablespoons butter, softened,
   divided**
**1 tablespoon instant espresso powder**
**1 teaspoon vanilla**
**1¾ cups all-purpose flour**
**½ teaspoon baking soda**
**½ teaspoon salt**
**¾ cup sugar**
**1 large egg**
**3 ounces imported Swiss white chocolate
   candy bar, broken**

**1.** Melt bittersweet chocolate and 2 tablespoons butter in small, heavy saucepan over low heat, stirring often. Add espresso powder; stir until dissolved. Remove from heat; stir in vanilla. Let cool to room temperature.

**2.** Combine flour, baking soda and salt in medium bowl.

**3.** Beat remaining ½ cup butter and sugar in large bowl with mixer at medium speed until fluffy. Beat in bittersweet chocolate mixture and egg. Gradually add flour mixture. Beat at low speed until well blended. Cover; refrigerate 30 minutes or until firm.

**4.** Preheat oven to 375°F. Roll tablespoonfuls of dough into 1-inch balls; place 3 inches apart on *ungreased* cookie sheets. Flatten each ball into ½-inch-thick round with fork dipped in sugar.

**5.** Bake 9 to 10 minutes or until set (do not overbake or cookies will become dry). Immediately remove cookies to wire racks; cool completely.

**6.** Place white chocolate in small resealable plastic freezer bag; seal bag. Microwave at MEDIUM (50% power) 1 minute. Turn bag over; microwave at MEDIUM 1 minute or until melted. Knead until chocolate is smooth. Cut off tiny corner of bag; pipe or drizzle white chocolate onto cooled cookies. Let stand 30 minutes or until set. Store tightly covered at room temperature or freeze up to 3 months.          *Makes about 4 dozen cookies*

## WALNUT MACAROONS

**2⅔ cups flaked coconut**
**1¼ cups coarsely chopped California walnuts**
**⅓ cup all-purpose flour**
**½ teaspoon ground cinnamon**
**¼ teaspoon salt**
**4 egg whites**
**1 teaspoon grated lemon peel**
**2 (1-ounce) squares semisweet chocolate,
   melted**

Combine coconut, walnuts, flour, cinnamon and salt in large bowl. Mix in egg whites and lemon peel. Drop by teaspoonfuls onto lightly greased cookie sheets. Bake at 325°F for 20 minutes or until golden brown. Dip macaroon bottoms in melted chocolate. Place on waxed paper to set.
*Makes about 3 dozen cookies*

*Favorite recipe from* **Walnut Marketing Board**

*Swiss Mocha Treats*

## ULTIMATE SUGAR COOKIES

**1¼ cups granulated sugar**
**1 CRISCO® Stick or 1 cup CRISCO®**
 **All-Vegetable Shortening**
**2 eggs**
**¼ cup light corn syrup or regular pancake**
 **syrup**
**1 tablespoon vanilla**
**3 cups all-purpose flour (plus**
 **4 tablespoons), divided**
**¾ teaspoon baking powder**
**½ teaspoon baking soda**
**½ teaspoon salt**
 **Granulated sugar or colored sugar**
 **crystals**

**1.** Place sugar and shortening in large bowl. Beat at medium speed of electric mixer until well blended. Add eggs, syrup and vanilla; beat until well blended and fluffy.

**2.** Combine 3 cups flour, baking powder, baking soda and salt in medium bowl. Add gradually to shortening mixture, beating at low speed until well blended.

**3.** Divide dough into 4 equal pieces; shape each piece into disk. Wrap with plastic wrap. Refrigerate 1 hour or until firm.

**4.** Preheat oven to 375°F. Place sheets of foil on countertop for cooling cookies.

**5.** Sprinkle about 1 tablespoon flour on large sheet of waxed paper. Place disk of dough on floured paper; flatten slightly with hands. Turn dough over; cover with another large sheet of waxed paper. Roll dough to ¼-inch thickness. Remove top sheet of waxed paper. Cut into desired shapes with floured cookie cutters. Place 2 inches apart on ungreased cookie sheet. Repeat with remaining dough.

**6.** Sprinkle with granulated sugar.

**7.** Bake one cookie sheet at a time at 375°F for 5 to 7 minutes or until edges of cookies are lightly browned. *Do not overbake.* Cool 2 minutes on cookie sheet. Remove cookies to foil to cool completely.          *Makes about 3½ dozen cookies*

*Ultimate Sugar Cookies*

COOKIE-JAR FAVORITES

## MAPLE WALNUT COOKIES

**1¼ cups firmly packed light brown sugar**
**¾ CRISCO® Stick or ¾ cup CRISCO®**
   **All-Vegetable Shortening**
**2 tablespoons maple syrup**
**1 teaspoon vanilla**
**1 teaspoon maple extract**
**1 egg**
**1¾ cups all-purpose flour**
**1 teaspoon salt**
**¾ teaspoon baking soda**
**½ teaspoon ground cinnamon**
**1½ cups chopped walnuts**
**30 to 40 walnut halves**

**1.** Preheat oven to 375°F. Place sheets of foil on countertop for cooling cookies.

**2.** Place brown sugar, shortening, maple syrup, vanilla and maple extract in large bowl. Beat at medium speed of electric mixer until well blended. Add egg; beat well.

**3.** Combine flour, salt, baking soda and cinnamon in small bowl. Add to shortening mixture; beat at low speed just until blended. Stir in chopped walnuts.

**4.** Drop dough by rounded measuring tablespoonfuls 3 inches apart onto ungreased cookie sheets. Press walnut half into center of each cookie.

**5.** Bake one cookie sheet at a time at 375°F for 8 to 10 minutes for chewy cookies, or 11 to 13 minutes for crisp cookies. *Do not overbake.* Cool 2 minutes on cookie sheet. Remove cookies to foil to cool completely.    *Makes about 3 dozen cookies*

## COCOA PECAN CRESCENTS

**1 cup (2 sticks) butter or margarine,**
   **softened**
**⅔ cup granulated sugar**
**1½ teaspoons vanilla extract**
**1¾ cups all-purpose flour**
**⅓ cup HERSHEY®S Cocoa**
**⅛ teaspoon salt**
**1½ cups ground pecans**
**Powdered sugar**

In large mixing bowl, beat butter, granulated sugar and vanilla until light and fluffy. Stir together flour, cocoa and salt in small bowl. Add to butter mixture; blend well. Stir in pecans. Refrigerate dough 1 hour or until firm enough to handle. Preheat oven to 375°F. Shape scant 1 tablespoon dough into log about 2½ inches long; place on ungreased cookie sheet. Shape each log into crescent, tapering ends. Bake 13 to 15 minutes or until set. Cool slightly; remove from cookie sheet to wire rack. Cool completely. Roll in powdered sugar.    *Makes about 3½ dozen cookies*

*Top to bottom: Maple Walnut Cookies,*
*Peanut Butter Treats (page 44)*

## CINNAMON-APRICOT TART OATMEAL COOKIES

  ½ **cup water**
  1 **package (8 ounces) dried apricot halves, diced**
  1 **CRISCO® Stick or 1 cup CRISCO® All-Vegetable Shortening**
  1 **cup firmly packed brown sugar**
  ¼ **cup granulated sugar**
  1 **egg**
  2 **teaspoons vanilla**
  1½ **cups all-purpose flour**
  2 **teaspoons ground cinnamon**
  1 **teaspoon baking soda**
  1 **teaspoon salt**
  1 **cup plus 2 tablespoons chopped pecans**
  3 **cups quick oats (not instant or old-fashioned)**

**1.** Place ½ cup water in small saucepan. Heat to boiling. Place diced apricots in strainer over boiling water. Reduce heat to low. Cover. Steam for 15 minutes. Cool. Reserve liquid.

**2.** Preheat oven to 375°F. Grease cookie sheet. Combine shortening, brown sugar, granulated sugar, egg and vanilla in large bowl. Beat at medium speed of electric mixer until well blended.

**3.** Combine flour, cinnamon, baking soda and salt in small bowl. Mix into creamed mixture at low speed until just blended. Stir in nuts, apricots and reserved liquid from apricots. Stir in oats with spoon. Drop rounded tablespoonfuls of dough 2 inches apart onto cookie sheet.

**4.** Bake at 375°F for 10 to 11 minutes. Cool 2 minutes on cookie sheet. Remove to wire rack. Cool completely.   *Makes 3½ to 4 dozen cookies*

## EASY LEMON COOKIES

  1 **package DUNCAN HINES® Moist Deluxe Lemon Cake Mix**
  2 **eggs**
  ½ **cup CRISCO® Oil**
  1 **teaspoon grated lemon peel**
   **Pecan halves, for garnish**

**1.** Preheat oven to 350°F.

**2.** Combine cake mix, eggs, oil and lemon peel in large bowl. Stir until thoroughly blended. Drop by rounded teaspoonfuls 2 inches apart onto ungreased cookie sheets. Press pecan half in center of each cookie. Bake at 350°F for 9 to 11 minutes or until edges are light golden brown. Cool 1 minute on cookie sheets. Remove to wire racks. Cool completely. Store in airtight container.

*Makes 4 dozen cookies*

**TIP:** You may substitute whole almonds or walnut halves for the pecan halves.

*Top to bottom: Chocolate-Orange Chip Cookies (page 48), Cinnamon-Apricot Tart Oatmeal Cookies*

## KENTUCKY BOURBON PECAN TARTS

    **Cream Cheese Pastry (recipe follows)**
**2 eggs**
**½ cup granulated sugar**
**½ cup KARO® Light or Dark Corn Syrup**
**2 tablespoons bourbon**
**1 tablespoon MAZOLA® Margarine, melted**
**½ teaspoon vanilla**
**1 cup chopped pecans**
    **Powdered sugar (optional)**

Preheat oven to 350°F. Prepare Cream Cheese Pastry. Divide dough in half; set aside one half. On floured surface, roll out pastry to ⅛-inch thickness. *If necessary, add small amount of flour to keep pastry from sticking.* Cut into 12 (2¼-inch) rounds. Press evenly into bottoms and up sides of 1¾-inch muffin pan cups. Repeat with remaining pastry. Refrigerate.

In medium bowl, beat eggs slightly. Stir in granulated sugar, corn syrup, bourbon, margarine and vanilla until well blended. Spoon 1 heaping teaspoon pecans into each pastry-lined cup; top with 1 tablespoon corn syrup mixture.

Bake 20 to 25 minutes or until lightly browned and toothpick inserted into center comes out clean. Cool in pans 5 minutes. Remove; cool completely on wire rack. If desired, sprinkle cookies with powdered sugar.
*Makes about 2 dozen cookies*

### CREAM CHEESE PASTRY

    **1 cup all-purpose flour**
**¾ teaspoon baking powder**
    **Pinch salt**
**½ cup MAZOLA® Margarine, softened**
**1 package (3 ounces) cream cheese, softened**
**2 teaspoons sugar**

In small bowl, combine flour, baking powder and salt. In large bowl, mix margarine, cream cheese and sugar until well combined. Stir in flour mixture until well blended. Press firmly into ball with hands.

**Prep Time:** 45 minutes
**Bake Time:** 25 minutes, plus cooling

*Top to bottom: Brandy Lace Cookies (page 30),*
*Kentucky Bourbon Pecan Tarts*

## AUSTRIAN TEA COOKIES

1½ cups sugar, divided
½ cup butter, softened
½ cup vegetable shortening
1 egg, beaten
½ teaspoon vanilla extract
2 cups all-purpose flour
2 cups ALMOND DELIGHT® Brand Cereal, crushed to 1 cup
½ teaspoon baking powder
¼ teaspoon ground cinnamon
14 ounces almond paste
2 egg whites
5 tablespoons raspberry or apricot jam, warmed

In large bowl, beat 1 cup sugar, butter and shortening. Add egg and vanilla; mix well. Stir in flour, cereal, baking powder and cinnamon until well blended. Refrigerate 1 to 2 hours or until firm.

Preheat oven to 350°F. Roll dough out on lightly floured surface to ¼-inch thickness; cut into 2-inch circles with floured cookie cutter. Place on ungreased cookie sheet; set aside. In small bowl, beat almond paste, egg whites and remaining ½ cup sugar until smooth. With pastry tube fitted with medium-sized star tip, pipe almond paste mixture ½ inch thick on top of each cookie along outside edge. Place ¼ teaspoon jam in center of each cookie, spreading out to paste. Bake 8 to 10 minutes or until lightly browned. Let stand 1 minute before removing from cookie sheet. Cool on wire rack.          *Makes about 3½ dozen cookies*

## BRANDY LACE COOKIES

¼ cup sugar
¼ cup MAZOLA® Margarine
¼ cup KARO® Light or Dark Corn Syrup
½ cup all-purpose flour
¼ cup very finely chopped pecans or walnuts
2 tablespoons brandy
Melted white and/or semisweet chocolate (optional)

Preheat oven to 350°F. Lightly grease and flour cookie sheets.

In small saucepan, combine sugar, margarine and corn syrup. Bring to boil over medium heat, stirring constantly. Remove from heat. Stir in flour, pecans and brandy. Drop 12 evenly spaced half teaspoonfuls of batter onto prepared cookie sheets.

Bake 6 minutes or until golden. Cool 1 to 2 minutes or until cookies can be lifted but are still warm and pliable; remove with spatula. Curl around handle of wooden spoon; slide off when crisp. If cookies harden before curling, return to oven to soften. If desired, drizzle with melted chocolate.          *Makes 4 to 5 dozen cookies*

**Prep Time:** 30 minutes
**Bake Time:** 6 minutes, plus curling and cooling

*Austrian Tea Cookies*

## PEANUT BUTTER SECRETS

**COOKIES**
   1  **CRISCO® Stick or 1 cup CRISCO®**
      **All-Vegetable Shortening**
   ¾ **cup firmly packed brown sugar**
   ½ **cup granulated sugar**
   ½ **cup JIF® Creamy Peanut Butter**
   1 **egg**
   1 **teaspoon vanilla**
   2 **cups all-purpose flour**
   1 **teaspoon baking soda**
   ½ **teaspoon salt**
  **40 to 45 chocolate-covered miniature peanut**
      **butter cups, unwrapped**

**GLAZE**
   1 **teaspoon CRISCO® All-Vegetable**
      **Shortening**
   1 **cup semi-sweet chocolate chips**
   2 **tablespoons JIF® Creamy Peanut Butter**

**1.** Preheat oven to 375°F. Grease cookie sheet with shortening.

**2. For Cookies,** combine shortening, brown sugar, granulated sugar and peanut butter in large bowl. Beat at medium speed of electric mixer until well blended. Beat in egg and vanilla.

**3.** Combine flour, baking soda and salt in small bowl. Mix into creamed mixture at low speed until just blended.

**4.** Form rounded teaspoonfuls of dough around each peanut butter cup. Enclose entirely. Place 2 inches apart on cookie sheet.

**5.** Bake 8 to 10 minutes or until cookies are just browned. Remove immediately to wire rack.

**6. For Glaze,** combine shortening, chocolate chips and peanut butter in microwave-safe cup. Microwave at 50% (MEDIUM). Stir after 1 minute. Repeat until smooth (or melt on rangetop in small saucepan on very low heat). Dip cookie tops in glaze.    *Makes about 3½ dozen cookies*

## QUICK CHOCOLATE MACAROONS

   1 **square BAKER'S® Unsweetened**
      **Chocolate**
  1⅓ **cups BAKER'S® ANGEL FLAKE® Coconut**
   ⅓ **cup sweetened condensed milk**
   ½ **teaspoon vanilla**

**HEAT** oven to 350°F.

**MELT** chocolate in large microwavable bowl on **HIGH** 1 to 2 minutes or until almost melted, stirring after each minute. **Stir until chocolate is completely melted.** Stir in coconut, condensed milk and vanilla. Drop from teaspoonfuls, 1 inch apart, onto well greased cookie sheets.

**BAKE** for 10 to 12 minutes or until set. Immediately remove from cookie sheets to cool on wire racks.    *Makes about 2 dozen cookies*

**Prep Time:** 10 minutes
**Baking Time:** 10 to 12 minutes

*Peanut Butter Secrets*

# CHIPS & CHUNKS

## PEANUT BUTTER CHOCOLATE CHIPPERS

**1 cup creamy or chunky peanut butter**
**1 cup firmly packed light brown sugar**
**1 large egg**
**¾ cup milk chocolate chips**
**Granulated sugar**

**1.** Preheat oven to 350°F.

**2.** Combine peanut butter, brown sugar and egg in medium bowl with mixing spoon until well blended. Add chips; mix well.

**3.** Roll heaping tablespoonfuls of dough into 1½-inch balls. Place balls 2 inches apart on *ungreased* cookie sheets.

**4.** Dip table fork into granulated sugar; press criss-cross fashion onto each ball, flattening to ½-inch thickness.

**5.** Bake 12 minutes or until set. Let cookies stand on cookie sheets 2 minutes. Remove cookies with spatula to wire racks; cool completely. Store tightly covered at room temperature or freeze up to 3 months. *Makes about 2 dozen cookies*

CHIPS & CHUNKS

## OATMEAL CANDIED CHIPPERS

¾ **cup all-purpose flour**
¾ **teaspoon salt**
½ **teaspoon baking soda**
¾ **cup butter or margarine, softened**
¾ **cup granulated sugar**
¾ **cup firmly packed light brown sugar**
3 **tablespoons milk**
1 **large egg**
2 **teaspoons vanilla**
3 **cups uncooked quick-cooking or old-fashioned oats**
1⅓ **cups (10-ounce package) candy-coated semisweet chocolate chips***

*Or, substitute 1 cup (8-ounce package) candy-coated milk chocolate chips.

**1.** Preheat oven to 375°F. Grease cookie sheets; set aside.

**2.** Combine flour, salt and baking soda in small bowl.

**3.** Beat butter, granulated sugar and brown sugar in large bowl with electric mixer at medium speed until light and fluffy. Add milk, egg and vanilla; beat well. Add flour mixture. Beat at low speed until blended. Stir in oats and chips.

**4.** Drop dough by tablespoonfuls 2 inches apart onto prepared cookie sheets.**

**Or, use a small ice cream scoop (#80) filled with dough and pressed against side of bowl to level.

**5.** Bake 10 to 11 minutes or until edges are golden brown. Let cookies stand 2 minutes on cookie sheets. Remove cookies with spatula to wire racks; cool completely. Store tightly covered at room temperature or freeze up to 3 months.

*Makes about 4 dozen cookies*

## CHOCOLATE-PEANUT COOKIES

1 **cup butter or margarine, softened**
¾ **cup granulated sugar**
¾ **cup firmly packed light brown sugar**
2 **eggs**
1 **teaspoon vanilla**
1 **teaspoon baking soda**
¼ **teaspoon salt**
2¼ **cups all-purpose flour**
2 **cups chocolate-covered peanuts**

Preheat oven to 375°F. Line cookie sheets with parchment paper or leave ungreased. Beat butter, granulated sugar, brown sugar, eggs and vanilla in large bowl with electric mixer until fluffy. Beat in baking soda and salt. Stir in flour to make stiff dough. Blend in chocolate-covered peanuts. Drop by rounded teaspoonfuls 2 inches apart onto cookie sheets. Bake 9 to 11 minutes or until just barely golden. *Do not overbake.* Remove to wire racks to cool. *Makes about 5 dozen cookies*

*Oatmeal Candied Chippers*

# CHOCOLATE CHIP SANDWICH COOKIES

**COOKIES**
1 package DUNCAN HINES® Chocolate Chip
    Cookie Mix
1 egg
⅓ cup CRISCO® Oil
3 tablespoons water

**CREAM FILLING**
1½ cups marshmallow creme
¾ cup butter or margarine, softened
2½ cups powdered sugar
1½ teaspoons vanilla extract

**1.** Preheat oven to 375°F.

**2. For Cookies,** combine cookie mix, egg, oil and water in large bowl. Stir until thoroughly blended. Drop by rounded teaspoonfuls 2 inches apart onto ungreased cookie sheets. Bake at 375°F for 8 to 10 minutes or until light golden brown. Cool 1 minute on cookie sheets. Remove to wire racks.

**3. For Cream Filling,** combine marshmallow creme and butter in large bowl. Add powdered sugar and vanilla extract, beating until smooth.

**4.** To assemble, spread bottoms of half the cookies with 1 tablespoon cream filling; top with remaining cookies. Press together to make sandwich cookies. Refrigerate to quickly firm the filling, if desired.

*Makes about 24 sandwich cookies*

**TIP:** After chilling the assembled cookies, wrap individually in plastic wrap. Store in the refrigerator until ready to serve.

# QUICK CHOCOLATE SOFTIES

1 package (18.25 ounces) devil's food
    chocolate cake mix
⅓ cup water
¼ cup butter or margarine, softened
1 large egg
1 cup large vanilla baking chips
½ cup coarsely chopped walnuts

**1.** Preheat oven to 350°F. Lightly grease cookie sheets.

**2.** Combine cake mix, water, butter and egg in large bowl. Beat with electric mixer at low speed until moistened. Increase speed to medium; beat 1 minute. (Dough will be thick.) Stir in chips and walnuts with mixing spoon until well blended.

**3.** Drop heaping *teaspoonfuls* of dough 2 inches apart (for smaller cookies) or heaping *tablespoonfuls* of dough 3 inches apart (for larger cookies) onto prepared cookie sheets.

**4.** Bake 10 to 12 minutes or until set. Let cookies stand on cookie sheets 1 minute. Remove cookies with spatula to wire racks; cool completely. Store tightly covered at room temperature or freeze up to 3 months.

*Makes about 2 dozen large or 4 dozen small cookies*

*Chocolate Chip Sandwich Cookies*

CHIPS & CHUNKS

# OATMEAL SCOTCHIES

1¼ **cups all-purpose flour**
1 **teaspoon baking soda**
½ **teaspoon salt**
½ **teaspoon ground cinnamon**
1 **cup (2 sticks) butter or margarine,
    softened**
¾ **cup granulated sugar**
¾ **cup packed brown sugar**
2 **eggs**
1 **teaspoon vanilla extract or grated peel of
    1 orange**
3 **cups quick *or* old-fashioned oats**
2 **cups (12-ounce package) NESTLÉ®
    TOLL HOUSE® Butterscotch Flavored
    Morsels**

**COMBINE** flour, baking soda, salt and cinnamon
in small bowl. Beat butter, granulated sugar, brown
sugar, eggs and vanilla in large mixing bowl until
creamy. Gradually beat in flour mixture. Stir in
oats and morsels. Drop by rounded tablespoons
onto ungreased cookie sheets.

**BAKE** in preheated 375°F oven for 7 to 8 minutes
for chewy cookies, 9 to 10 minutes for crisp
cookies. Let stand for 2 minutes; remove to wire
racks to cool completely. *Makes 4 dozen cookies*

# CHOCO-SCUTTERBOTCH

⅔ **CRISCO® Stick or ⅔ cup CRISCO®
    All-Vegetable Shortening**
½ **cup firmly packed brown sugar**
2 **eggs**
1 **package DUNCAN HINES® Moist Deluxe
    Yellow Cake Mix**
1 **cup toasted rice cereal**
½ **cup milk chocolate chunks**
½ **cup butterscotch chips**
½ **cup semi-sweet chocolate chips**
½ **cup coarsely chopped walnuts or pecans**

**1.** Preheat oven to 375°F.

**2.** Combine shortening and brown sugar in large
bowl. Beat at medium speed of electric mixer until
well blended. Beat in eggs.

**3.** Add cake mix gradually at low speed. Mix until
well blended. Stir in cereal, chocolate chunks,
butterscotch chips, chocolate chips and nuts with
spoon until well blended. Shape dough into
1¼-inch balls. Place 2 inches apart on ungreased
cookie sheet. Flatten slightly. Shape sides to form
circle, if necessary.

**4.** Bake at 375°F for 7 to 9 minutes or until lightly
browned around edges. Cool 2 minutes before
removing to paper towels to cool completely.
*Makes about 3 dozen cookies*

*Oatmeal Scotchies*

## ORIGINAL NESTLÉ® TOLL HOUSE® CHOCOLATE CHIP COOKIES

2¼ cups all-purpose flour
1 teaspoon baking soda
1 teaspoon salt
1 cup (2 sticks) butter, softened
¾ cup granulated sugar
¾ cup firmly packed brown sugar
1 teaspoon vanilla extract
2 eggs
2 cups (12-ounce package) NESTLÉ® TOLL HOUSE® Semi-Sweet Chocolate Morsels
1 cup chopped nuts

COMBINE flour, baking soda and salt in small bowl. Beat butter, granulated sugar, brown sugar and vanilla in large mixing bowl. Add eggs one at a time, beating well after each addition; gradually beat in flour mixture. Stir in morsels and nuts. Drop by rounded tablespoons onto ungreased cookie sheets.

BAKE in preheated 375°F oven for 9 to 11 minutes or until golden brown. Let stand for 2 minutes; remove to wire racks to cool completely.

*Makes about 5 dozen cookies*

## COWBOY COOKIES

½ cup butter or margarine, softened
½ cup firmly packed light brown sugar
¼ cup granulated sugar
1 egg
1 teaspoon vanilla
1 cup all-purpose flour
2 tablespoons unsweetened cocoa
½ teaspoon baking powder
¼ teaspoon baking soda
1 cup uncooked rolled oats
1 cup (6 ounces) semisweet chocolate chips
½ cup raisins
½ cup chopped nuts

Preheat oven to 375°F. Lightly grease cookie sheets or line with parchment paper. Beat butter, brown sugar and granulated sugar in large bowl with electric mixer until blended. Add egg and vanilla; beat until fluffy. Combine flour, cocoa, baking powder and baking soda in small bowl; stir into creamed mixture with oats, chocolate chips, raisins and nuts. Drop dough by teaspoonfuls 2 inches apart onto prepared cookie sheets. Bake 10 to 12 minutes or until lightly browned around edges. Remove to wire racks to cool.

*Makes about 4 dozen cookies*

*Original Nestlé® Toll House® Chocolate Chip Cookies*

## WHOLE GRAIN CHIPPERS

**1 cup butter or margarine, softened**
**1 cup firmly packed light brown sugar**
**⅔ cup granulated sugar**
**2 eggs**
**1 teaspoon baking soda**
**1 teaspoon vanilla**
   **Pinch salt**
**1 cup whole wheat flour**
**1 cup all-purpose flour**
**2 cups uncooked rolled oats**
**1 package (12 ounces) semisweet chocolate
   chips**
**1 cup sunflower seeds**

Preheat oven to 375°F. Lightly grease cookie sheets or line with parchment paper. Beat butter, brown sugar, granulated sugar and eggs in large bowl with electric mixer until light and fluffy. Beat in baking soda, vanilla and salt. Blend in flours and oats to make a stiff dough. Stir in chocolate chips. Shape rounded teaspoonfuls of dough into balls; roll in sunflower seeds. Place 2 inches apart on prepared cookie sheets. Bake 8 to 10 minutes or until firm. *Do not overbake.* Cool a few minutes on cookie sheets, then remove to wire racks to cool completely.                        *Makes about 6 dozen cookies*

## PEANUT BUTTER TREATS

**1¼ cups firmly packed light brown sugar**
**¾ CRISCO® Stick or ¾ cup CRISCO®
   All-Vegetable Shortening**
**2 tablespoons milk**
**1 tablespoon vanilla**
**1 egg**
**1¾ cups all-purpose flour**
**1 teaspoon salt**
**¾ teaspoon baking soda**
**2 cups (about 32) miniature peanut butter
   cups, unwrapped and quartered or
   coarsely chopped**

**1.** Preheat oven to 375°F. Place sheets of foil on countertop for cooling cookies.

**2.** Place brown sugar, shortening, milk and vanilla in large bowl. Beat at medium speed of electric mixer until well blended. Add egg; beat well.

**3.** Combine flour, salt and baking soda in small bowl. Add to shortening mixture; beat at low speed just until blended. Stir in peanut butter cup quarters.

**4.** Drop dough by rounded measuring tablespoonfuls 3 inches apart onto ungreased cookie sheets.

**5.** Bake one cookie sheet at a time at 375°F for 8 to 10 minutes or until cookies are lightly browned. *Do not overbake.* Cool 2 minutes on cookie sheet. Remove cookies to foil to cool completely.
*Makes about 3 dozen cookies*

*Whole Grain Chippers*

CHIPS & CHUNKS

# BUTTER-FLAVORED BRICKLE DRIZZLES

## COOKIES
1 CRISCO® Stick or 1 cup CRISCO®
   All-Vegetable Shortening
1 cup granulated sugar
1 cup firmly packed brown sugar
1 can (14 ounces) sweetened condensed
   milk (not evaporated milk)
1 teaspoon vanilla
1¾ cups all-purpose flour
1 teaspoon salt
½ teaspoon baking soda
3 cups quick oats, uncooked
1 cup almond brickle chips

## DRIZZLE
1 cup milk chocolate chips

**1.** Preheat oven to 350°F. Grease cookie sheet.

**2. For Cookies,** combine shortening, granulated sugar and brown sugar in large bowl. Stir with spoon until well blended and creamy. Stir in condensed milk and vanilla. Mix well.

**3.** Combine flour, salt and baking soda in small bowl. Stir into creamed mixture. Stir in oats.

**4.** Shape dough into 1-inch balls. Press tops into brickle chips. Place, brickle side up, 2 inches apart on greased cookie sheet.

**5.** Bake at 350°F for 9 to 10 minutes or until set but not browned. Remove to wire rack. Cool completely.

**6. For Drizzle,** place chocolate chips in heavy resealable sandwich bag. Seal. Microwave at 50% (MEDIUM). Knead bag after 1 minute. Repeat until smooth (or melt by placing in bowl of hot water). Cut tiny tip off bottom corner of bag. Squeeze out and drizzle over cookies.

*Makes about 6 dozen cookies*

*Butter-Flavored Brickle Drizzles*

## IVORY CHIP STRAWBERRY FUDGE DROPS

**⅔ CRISCO® Stick or ⅔ cup CRISCO®
    All-Vegetable Shortening**
**1 cup sugar**
**1 egg**
**½ teaspoon strawberry extract**
**½ cup buttermilk**
**6 tablespoons puréed frozen sweetened
    strawberries**
**1¾ cups all-purpose flour**
**6 tablespoons unsweetened cocoa powder**
**¾ teaspoon baking soda**
**½ teaspoon salt**
**1½ cups white chocolate baking chips**

**1.** Preheat oven to 350°F. Grease cookie sheet. Combine shortening, sugar, egg and strawberry extract in large bowl. Beat at medium speed of electric mixer until well blended. Beat in buttermilk and strawberry purée.

**2.** Combine flour, cocoa, baking soda and salt in medium bowl. Mix into creamed mixture at low speed of electric mixer until blended. Stir in white chocolate chips.

**3.** Drop rounded tablespoonfuls of dough 2 inches apart onto cookie sheet.

**4.** Bake 11 to 12 minutes or until tops spring back when pressed lightly. Remove immediately to wire rack. Cool completely.

*Makes about 2½ dozen cookies*

## CHOCOLATE-ORANGE CHIP COOKIES

**½ CRISCO® Stick or ½ cup CRISCO®
    All-Vegetable Shortening**
**1¼ cups firmly packed brown sugar**
**2 squares (1 ounce each) unsweetened
    chocolate, melted and cooled**
**1 egg**
**2 tablespoons orange juice concentrate**
**2 tablespoons grated orange peel**
**1 teaspoon vanilla**
**1½ cups all-purpose flour**
**¾ teaspoon baking soda**
**¼ teaspoon salt**
**1 cup semi-sweet chocolate chips**
**½ cup blanched slivered almonds**

**1.** Preheat oven to 375°F. Combine shortening, sugar and melted chocolate in large bowl. Beat at medium speed of electric mixer until well blended. Beat in egg, concentrate, peel and vanilla.

**2.** Combine flour, baking soda and salt in small bowl. Mix into creamed mixture at low speed until well blended. Stir in chocolate chips and nuts.

**3.** Drop tablespoonfuls of dough 2 inches apart onto ungreased cookie sheet.

**4.** Bake at 375°F for 7 to 9 minutes or until set. Cool 2 minutes on cookie sheet. Remove to wire rack. Cool completely.

*Makes about 3½ dozen cookies*

*Ivory Chip Strawberry Fudge Drops*

## ULTIMATE CHOCOLATE CHIP COOKIES

**¾ CRISCO® Stick or ¾ cup CRISCO®**
   **All-Vegetable Shortening**
**1¼ cups firmly packed brown sugar**
   **2 tablespoons milk**
   **1 tablespoon vanilla**
   **1 egg**
**1¾ cups all-purpose flour**
   **1 teaspoon salt**
   **¾ teaspoon baking soda**
   **1 cup semi-sweet chocolate chips**
   **1 cup coarsely chopped pecans***

*You may substitute an additional ½ cup semi-sweet chocolate chips for the pecans.

1. Preheat oven to 375°F.

2. Combine shortening, sugar, milk and vanilla in large bowl. Beat at medium speed of electric mixer until well blended. Beat in egg.

3. Combine flour, salt and baking soda in small bowl. Mix into creamed mixture at low speed until just blended. Stir in chocolate chips and nuts.

4. Drop rounded tablespoonfuls of dough 3 inches apart onto ungreased cookie sheet.

5. Bake at 375°F for 8 to 10 minutes for chewy cookies (they will look light and moist—*do not overbake*), 11 to 13 minutes for crisp cookies. Cool 2 minutes on cookie sheet. Remove to wire rack. Cool completely.       *Makes about 3 dozen cookies*

**Variations for Ultimate Chocolate Chip Cookies**

**DRIZZLE:** Combine 1 teaspoon CRISCO® All-Vegetable Shortening and 1 cup semi-sweet chocolate chips or 1 cup white melting chocolate, cut into small pieces, in microwave-safe measuring cup. Microwave at 50% (MEDIUM). Stir after 1 minute. Repeat until smooth (or melt on rangetop in small saucepan on very low heat). To thin, add a little more shortening. Drizzle back and forth over cookie. Sprinkle with nuts before chocolate hardens, if desired. To quickly harden chocolate, place cookies in refrigerator for a few minutes.

**CHOCOLATE DIPPED:** Melt chocolate as directed for Drizzle. Dip one end of cooled cookie halfway up in chocolate. Sprinkle with finely chopped nuts before chocolate hardens. Place on waxed paper until chocolate is firm. To quickly harden chocolate, place cookies in refrigerator for a few minutes.

*Clockwise from top: Old-Fashioned Oatmeal Cookies (page 14),*
*Peanut Butter Sensations (page 6),*
*Ultimate Chocolate Chip Cookies*

# — *Keepsake* —

# BAR COOKIES

### CHOCOLATE CHIP SHORTBREAD

½ **cup butter, softened**
½ **cup sugar**
1 **teaspoon vanilla**
1 **cup all-purpose flour**
¼ **teaspoon salt**
½ **cup mini semisweet chocolate chips**

Preheat oven to 375°F. Beat butter and sugar in large bowl with electric mixer at medium speed until light and fluffy. Beat in vanilla. Add flour and salt. Stir in chips.

Divide dough in half. Press each half into ungreased 8-inch round cake pan. Bake 12 minutes or until edges are golden brown. Score shortbread with sharp knife, taking care not to cut completely through shortbread. Make 8 wedges per pan.

Let pans stand on wire racks 10 minutes. Invert shortbread onto wire racks; cool completely. Break into wedges. *Makes 16 cookies*

# BAR COOKIES

## PEANUT BUTTER BARS

½ CRISCO® Stick or ½ cup CRISCO®
   All-Vegetable Shortening
1½ cups firmly packed brown sugar
⅔ cup JIF® Creamy or Extra Crunchy Peanut
   Butter
2 eggs
1 teaspoon vanilla
1½ cups all-purpose flour
½ teaspoon salt
¼ cup milk

**1.** Preheat oven to 350°F. Grease 13×9×2-inch baking pan.

**2.** Combine shortening, brown sugar and peanut butter in large bowl. Beat at medium speed of electric mixer until well blended. Beat in eggs and vanilla.

**3.** Combine flour and salt in small bowl. Add alternately with milk to creamed mixture at low speed. Beat until well blended. Spread in pan.

**4.** Bake 28 to 32 minutes or until golden brown and center is set. Cool in pan on wire rack. Top with frosting or glaze, if desired. Cut into 2¼×1½-inch bars.          *Makes 32 bars*

**Frosting and Glaze Variations**

**CHOCOLATE DREAM FROSTING:**
Combine 2 tablespoons CRISCO® All-Vegetable Shortening, 1 cup miniature marshmallows, 1 square (1 ounce) unsweetened chocolate and 3 tablespoons milk in medium microwave-safe bowl. Cover with waxed paper. Microwave at 50% (MEDIUM). Stir after 1 minute. Repeat until smooth (or melt on rangetop in medium saucepan on low heat). Stir in 1¾ cups powdered sugar. Beat until well blended. Spread over top. Sprinkle ¼ cup finely chopped peanuts over frosting. Set aside until frosting is firm. Cut into bars.

**MICROWAVE CHOCOLATE CHIP GLAZE:**
Combine 1 tablespoon CRISCO® All-Vegetable Shortening, ¼ cup semi-sweet chocolate chips and 3 tablespoons milk in medium microwave-safe bowl. Microwave at 50% (MEDIUM). Stir after 1 minute. Repeat until smooth (or melt on rangetop in small saucepan on very low heat). Add ½ cup powdered sugar and ¼ teaspoon vanilla. Stir until smooth. (Add small amount of hot milk if thinner consistency is desired.) Drizzle over top. Sprinkle ¼ cup finely chopped peanuts over glaze. Set aside until glaze is firm. Cut into bars.

*Top to bottom: "Cordially Yours" Chocolate Chip Bars (page 56),*
*Peanut Butter Bars*

## CALIFORNIA APRICOT POWER BARS

**2 cups California dried apricot halves, coarsely chopped (12 ounces)**
**2½ cups pecans, coarsely chopped (10 ounces)**
**1¼ cups pitted dates, coarsely chopped (8 ounces)**
**1¼ cups whole wheat flour**
**1 teaspoon baking powder**
**1 cup firmly packed brown sugar**
**3 large eggs**
**¼ cup apple juice or water**
**1½ teaspoons vanilla**

Preheat oven to 350°F. Line 15½×10½×1-inch jelly-roll pan with foil. In large bowl, stir together apricots, pecans and dates; divide in half. In small bowl, combine flour and baking powder; add to half of fruit-nut mixture. Toss to coat. In medium bowl, combine brown sugar, eggs, apple juice and vanilla; stir into flour mixture until thoroughly moistened. Spread batter evenly into prepared pan. Lightly press remaining fruit-nut mixture on top.

Bake 20 minutes or until bars are golden and spring back when pressed lightly. Cool in pan 5 minutes. Turn out onto wire rack; cool 45 minutes. Peel off foil and cut into bars. Store in airtight container. Bars may be frozen.

*Makes about 32 bars*

*Favorite recipe from **California Apricot Advisory Board***

## "CORDIALLY YOURS" CHOCOLATE CHIP BARS

**¾ CRISCO® Stick or ¾ cup CRISCO® All-Vegetable Shortening**
**2 eggs**
**½ cup granulated sugar**
**¼ cup firmly packed brown sugar**
**1½ teaspoons vanilla**
**1 teaspoon almond extract**
**2 cups all-purpose flour**
**1 teaspoon baking soda**
**½ teaspoon ground cinnamon**
**1 can (21 ounces) cherry pie filling**
**1½ cups milk chocolate big chips**
**Powdered sugar**

**1.** Preheat oven to 350°F. Grease 15½×10½×1-inch jelly-roll pan.

**2.** Combine shortening, eggs, granulated sugar, brown sugar, vanilla and almond extract in large bowl. Beat at medium speed of electric mixer until well blended.

**3.** Combine flour, baking soda and cinnamon in medium bowl. Mix into creamed mixture at low speed until just blended. Stir in pie filling and chocolate chips. Spread in pan.

**4.** Bake 25 minutes or until lightly browned and top springs back when lightly pressed. Cool completely in pan on wire rack. Sprinkle with powdered sugar. Cut into 2½×2-inch bars.

*Makes 30 bars*

*California Apricot Power Bars*

*BAR COOKIES*

## LAYERED CHOCOLATE CHEESE BARS

¼ cup (½ stick) margarine or butter
1½ cups graham cracker crumbs
¾ cup sugar
1 package (4 ounces) BAKER'S®
    GERMAN'S® Sweet Chocolate, melted
1 package (8 ounces) PHILADELPHIA
    BRAND® Cream Cheese, softened
1 egg
1 cup BAKER'S® ANGEL FLAKE® Coconut
1 cup chopped nuts

**HEAT** oven to 350°F.

**MELT** margarine in oven in 13×9-inch pan. Add graham cracker crumbs and ¼ cup of the sugar; mix well. Press into pan. Bake for 10 minutes.

**COMBINE** melted chocolate, the remaining ½ cup sugar, the cream cheese and egg. Spread over crust. Sprinkle with coconut and nuts; press lightly.

**BAKE** for 30 minutes. Cool; cut into bars.

*Makes about 24 bars*

**Prep Time:** 20 minutes
**Baking Time:** 40 minutes

## BANANA SPLIT BARS

⅓ cup margarine or butter, softened
1 cup sugar
1 egg
1 banana, mashed
½ teaspoon vanilla
1¼ cups all-purpose flour
1 teaspoon CALUMET® Baking Powder
¼ teaspoon salt
⅓ cup chopped nuts
2 cups KRAFT® Miniature Marshmallows
1 cup BAKER'S® Semi-Sweet Real
    Chocolate Chips
⅓ cup maraschino cherries, drained and
    quartered

**HEAT** oven to 350°F.

**BEAT** margarine and sugar until light and fluffy. Add egg, banana and vanilla; mix well. Mix in flour, baking powder and salt. Stir in nuts. Pour into greased 13×9-inch pan.

**BAKE** for 20 minutes. Remove from oven. Sprinkle with marshmallows, chips and cherries. Bake 10 to 15 minutes longer or until toothpick inserted in center comes out clean. Cool in pan; cut into bars.

*Makes about 24 bars*

**Prep Time:** 20 minutes
**Baking Time:** 30 to 35 minutes

*Top plate (clockwise from top): Layered Chocolate Cheese Bar, Banana Split Bar, Chocolate Peanut Butter Bar (page 68)*

# BAR COOKIES

## PEACHY OATMEAL BARS

**CRUMB MIXTURE**
1½ cups all-purpose flour
1 cup uncooked rolled oats
¾ cup margarine, melted
½ cup sugar
2 teaspoons almond extract
½ teaspoon baking soda
¼ teaspoon salt

**FILLING**
¾ cup peach or apricot preserves
⅓ cup flaked coconut

Preheat oven to 350°F.

**For Crumb Mixture,** combine all crumb mixture ingredients in large bowl of electric mixer. Beat at low speed, scraping bowl often, until mixture is crumbly, 1 to 2 minutes. *Reserve ¾ cup crumb mixture;* press remaining crumb mixture onto bottom of greased 9-inch square baking pan.

**For Filling,** spread preserves to within ½ inch of edge of crust; sprinkle with reserved crumb mixture and coconut. Bake for 20 to 25 minutes or until edges are lightly browned. Cool completely. Cut into bars.       *Makes about 24 bars*

## STREUSEL STRAWBERRY BARS

1 cup butter or margarine, softened
1 cup sugar
2 cups all-purpose flour
1 egg
¾ cup pecans, coarsely chopped
1 jar (10 ounces) strawberry or raspberry preserves

Preheat oven to 350°F. Combine butter and sugar in large mixing bowl. Beat at low speed, scraping bowl often, until well blended. Add flour and egg. Beat until mixture is crumbly, 2 to 3 minutes. Stir in pecans. Reserve 1 cup crumb mixture; press remaining crumb mixture onto bottom of greased 9-inch square baking pan. Spread preserves to within ½ inch of edge of crust. Crumble reserved crumb mixture over preserves. Bake for 40 to 50 minutes or until lightly browned. Cool completely. Cut into bars.       *Makes about 24 bars*

*Top to bottom: Peachy Oatmeal Bars, Streusel Strawberry Bars*

## BAR COOKIES

## CHOCOLATE CARAMEL PECAN BARS

   **2 cups butter, softened, divided**
   **½ cup granulated sugar**
   **1 large egg**
   **2¾ cups all-purpose flour**
   **⅔ cup firmly packed light brown sugar**
   **¼ cup light corn syrup**
   **2½ cups coarsely chopped pecans**
   **1 cup semisweet chocolate chips**

**1.** Preheat oven to 375°F. Grease 15×10-inch jelly-roll pan; set aside.

**2.** Beat 1 cup butter and granulated sugar in large bowl with electric mixer at medium speed until light and fluffy. Beat in egg. Add flour. Beat at low speed until blended. Pat dough into prepared pan.

**3.** Bake 20 minutes or until light golden brown.

**4.** While bars are baking, prepare topping. Combine remaining 1 cup butter, brown sugar and corn syrup in medium, heavy saucepan. Cook over medium heat until mixture boils, stirring frequently. Boil gently 2 minutes, without stirring. Quickly stir in pecans and spread topping evenly over base. Return to oven and bake 20 minutes or until dark golden brown and bubbling.

**5.** Immediately sprinkle chocolate chips evenly over hot caramel. Gently press chips into caramel topping with spatula. Loosen caramel from edges of pan with a thin spatula or knife.

**6.** Remove pan to wire rack; cool completely. Cut into 3×1½-inch bars. Store tightly covered at room temperature or freeze up to 3 months.

*Makes 40 bars*

## ALMOND TOFFEE SQUARES

   **1 cup (2 sticks) margarine or butter, softened**
   **1 cup firmly packed brown sugar**
   **1 egg**
   **1 teaspoon vanilla**
   **2 cups all-purpose flour**
   **¼ teaspoon salt**
   **2 packages (4 ounces each) BAKER'S® GERMAN'S® Sweet Chocolate, broken into squares**
   **½ cup toasted slivered almonds**
   **½ cup lightly toasted BAKER'S® ANGEL FLAKE® Coconut**

**HEAT** oven to 350°F.

**BEAT** margarine, sugar, egg and vanilla. Mix in flour and salt. Press into greased 13×9-inch pan.

**BAKE** for 30 minutes or until edges are golden brown. Remove from oven. Immediately sprinkle with chocolate squares. Cover with foil; let stand 5 minutes or until chocolate is softened.

**SPREAD** chocolate evenly over entire surface; sprinkle with almonds and coconut. Cut into squares while still warm. Cool on wire rack.

*Makes about 26 squares*

*Chocolate Caramel Pecan Bars*

## LEMON NUT BARS

1⅓ cups all-purpose flour
½ cup firmly packed brown sugar
¼ cup granulated sugar
¾ cup butter
1 cup old-fashioned or quick oats, uncooked
½ cup chopped nuts
1 (8-ounce) package PHILADELPHIA BRAND® Cream Cheese, softened
1 egg
3 tablespoons lemon juice
1 tablespoon grated lemon peel

Preheat oven to 350°F. Stir together flour and sugars in medium bowl. Cut in butter until mixture resembles coarse crumbs. Stir in oats and nuts. Reserve 1 cup crumb mixture; press remaining crumb mixture onto bottom of greased 13×9-inch baking pan. Bake 15 minutes. Beat cream cheese, egg, juice and peel in small mixing bowl at medium speed with electric mixer until well blended. Pour over crust; sprinkle with reserved crumb mixture. Bake 25 minutes. Cool; cut into bars. *Makes about 36 bars*

**Prep Time:** 30 minutes
**Cook Time:** 25 minutes

## CHOCOLATE PECAN PIE BARS

1⅓ cups all-purpose flour
2 tablespoons plus ½ cup firmly packed light brown sugar, divided
½ cup (1 stick) cold butter or margarine
2 eggs
½ cup light corn syrup
¼ cup HERSHEY®S Cocoa
2 tablespoons butter or margarine, melted
1 teaspoon vanilla extract
⅛ teaspoon salt
1 cup coarsely chopped pecans

Preheat oven to 350°F. In large bowl, stir together flour and 2 tablespoons brown sugar. With pastry blender, cut in ½ cup butter until mixture resembles coarse crumbs; press onto bottom and about 1 inch up sides of ungreased 9-inch square baking pan. Bake 10 to 12 minutes or until set. Remove from oven. With back of spoon, lightly press crust into corners and against sides of pan. In small bowl, lightly beat eggs, corn syrup, remaining ½ cup brown sugar, cocoa, 2 tablespoons butter, vanilla and salt until well blended. Stir in pecans. Pour mixture over warm crust. Continue baking 25 minutes or until pecan filling is set. Cool completely in pan on wire rack. Cut into bars. *Makes about 16 bars*

*Lemon Nut Bars*

## BAR COOKIES

## CHUNKY MACADAMIA BARS

¾ **cup (1½ sticks) butter or margarine, softened**
1 **cup firmly packed light brown sugar**
½ **cup granulated sugar**
1 **egg**
1 **teaspoon vanilla extract**
2¼ **cups all-purpose flour**
1 **teaspoon baking soda**
¾ **cup coarsely chopped macadamia nuts**
1¾ **cups (10-ounce package) HERSHEY®S Semi-Sweet Chocolate Chunks, divided**
**Quick Vanilla Glaze (recipe follows)**

Preheat oven to 375°F. In large mixing bowl, beat butter, brown sugar and granulated sugar until creamy. Add egg and vanilla; beat well. Add flour and baking soda; blend well. Stir in nuts and 1 cup chocolate chunks. Press dough onto bottom of ungreased 13×9×2-inch baking pan. Sprinkle with remaining ¾ cup chocolate chunks. Bake 22 to 25 minutes or until golden brown. Cool completely in pan on wire rack. Prepare Quick Vanilla Glaze; drizzle over top of bars. Allow glaze to set. Cut into bars.      *Makes about 24 bars*

### QUICK VANILLA GLAZE
1 **cup powdered sugar**
2 **tablespoons milk**
½ **teaspoon vanilla extract**

In small bowl, combine powdered sugar, milk and vanilla; stir until smooth and of desired consistency.

## CHOCOLATE AMARETTO SQUARES

½ **cup (1 stick) butter (do *not* use margarine), melted**
1 **cup sugar**
2 **eggs**
½ **cup all-purpose flour**
⅓ **cup HERSHEY®S Cocoa or HERSHEY®S European Style Cocoa**
2 **tablespoons almond flavored liqueur *or*
½ teaspoon almond extract**
1¼ **cups ground almonds**
**Sliced almonds (optional)**

Preheat oven to 325°F. Grease 8-inch square baking pan. In large bowl, beat butter and sugar until creamy. Add eggs, flour and cocoa; beat well. Stir in almond liqueur and ground almonds. Pour batter into prepared pan. Bake 35 to 40 minutes or just until set. Cool completely in pan on wire rack. Cut into squares. Garnish with sliced almonds, if desired.      *Makes about 16 squares*

*Clockwise from top: Chunky Macadamia Bars, Chocolate Amaretto Squares, Chocolate Pecan Pie Bars (page 64)*

## HEATH® BARS

**1 cup butter, softened**
**1 cup firmly packed brown sugar**
**1 egg yolk**
**1 teaspoon vanilla**
**2 cups all-purpose flour**
**18 to 19 Original HEATH® English Toffee
     Snack Size Bars, crushed, divided**
**½ cup finely chopped pecans**

Preheat oven to 350°F. In large bowl, with electric mixer, beat butter well; blend in brown sugar, egg yolk and vanilla. By hand, mix in flour, ⅔ cup Heath® Bars and nuts. Press into ungreased 15½×10½-inch jelly-roll pan.

Bake 18 to 20 minutes or until browned. Remove from oven and immediately sprinkle remaining Heath® Bars over top. Cool slightly; cut into bars while warm.          *Makes about 48 bars*

## CHOCOLATE PEANUT BUTTER BARS

**2 cups peanut butter**
**1 cup sugar**
**2 eggs**
**1 package (8 ounces) BAKER'S®
     Semi-Sweet Chocolate**
**1 cup chopped peanuts**

**HEAT** oven to 350°F.

**BEAT** peanut butter, sugar and eggs in large bowl until light and fluffy. Reserve 1 cup peanut butter mixture; set aside.

**MELT** four squares of the chocolate. Add to peanut butter mixture in bowl; mix well. Press into ungreased 13×9-inch pan. Top with reserved peanut butter mixture.

**BAKE** for 30 minutes or until edges are lightly browned. Melt the remaining 4 squares chocolate; spread evenly over entire surface. Sprinkle with peanuts. Cool in pan until chocolate is set. Cut into bars.          *Makes about 24 bars*

**Prep Time:** 15 minutes
**Baking Time:** 30 minutes

*Heath® Bars*

## LUSCIOUS LEMON BARS

**CRUST**
  ½ cup butter or margarine, softened
  ½ cup granulated sugar
    Grated peel of ½ SUNKIST® Lemon
1¼ cups all-purpose flour

**LEMON LAYER**
  4 eggs
1⅔ cups granulated sugar
  3 tablespoons all-purpose flour
  ½ teaspoon baking powder
    Grated peel of ½ SUNKIST® Lemon
    Juice of 2 SUNKIST® Lemons
      (6 tablespoons)
  1 teaspoon vanilla extract
    Powdered sugar

**For Crust,** in medium bowl, cream together butter, granulated sugar and lemon peel. Gradually stir in flour to form a soft crumbly dough. Press evenly into bottom of aluminum foil-lined 13×9×2-inch baking pan. Bake at 350° for 15 minutes.

**For Lemon Layer,** while crust is baking, in large bowl, whisk or beat eggs well. Stir together granulated sugar, flour and baking powder. Gradually whisk sugar mixture into eggs. Whisk in lemon peel, juice and vanilla. Pour over hot crust. Return to oven. Bake for 20 to 25 minutes or until top is lightly browned. Cool. Using foil on two sides, lift out cookie base. Gently loosen foil along all sides. With long wet knife, cut into bars or squares. Sprinkle tops with powdered sugar.

*Makes about 3 dozen bars*

## BLUEBERRY CHEESECAKE BARS

  1 package DUNCAN HINES® Blueberry
    Muffin Mix
¼ cup butter or margarine, softened
⅓ cup finely chopped pecans
  1 package (8 ounces) cream cheese,
    softened
½ cup sugar
  1 egg
  3 tablespoons lemon juice
  1 teaspoon grated lemon peel

**1.** Preheat oven to 350°F. Grease 9-inch square baking pan.

**2.** Rinse blueberries from Mix with cold water and drain.

**3.** Place muffin mix in medium bowl. Cut in butter with pastry blender or two knives. Stir in pecans. Press into bottom of pan. Bake at 350°F for 15 minutes or until set.

**4.** Combine cream cheese and sugar in medium bowl. Beat until smooth. Add egg, lemon juice and lemon peel. Beat well. Spread over baked crust. Sprinkle with blueberries. Sprinkle topping packet from Mix over blueberries. Return to oven. Bake at 350°F for 35 to 40 minutes or until filling is set. Cool completely. Refrigerate until ready to serve. Cut into bars.

*Makes 16 bars*

*Blueberry Cheesecake Bars*

**BAR COOKIES**

# TRIPLE LAYER PEANUT BUTTER BARS

## BASE
1¼ cups firmly packed light brown sugar
¾ cup creamy peanut butter
½ CRISCO® Stick or ½ cup CRISCO®
    All-Vegetable Shortening
3 tablespoons milk
1 tablespoon vanilla
1 egg
1¾ cups all-purpose flour
¾ teaspoon baking soda
¾ teaspoon salt

## PEANUT BUTTER LAYER
1½ cups powdered sugar
2 tablespoons creamy peanut butter
1 tablespoon CRISCO® All-Vegetable
    Shortening
3 tablespoons milk

## CHOCOLATE GLAZE
2 squares (1 ounce each) unsweetened
    baking chocolate
2 tablespoons CRISCO® All-Vegetable
    Shortening

**1.** Preheat oven to 350°F. Grease 13×9-inch baking pan. Place wire rack on countertop.

**2. For Base,** place brown sugar, peanut butter, shortening, milk and vanilla in large bowl. Beat at medium speed of electric mixer until well blended. Add egg; beat just until blended.

**3.** Combine flour, baking soda and salt in small bowl. Add to shortening mixture; beat at low speed just until blended.

**4.** Press mixture onto bottom of prepared pan.

**5.** Bake at 350°F for 18 to 20 minutes or until wooden pick inserted in center comes out clean. *Do not overbake.* Cool completely on wire rack.

**6. For Peanut Butter Layer,** place powdered sugar, peanut butter, shortening and milk in medium bowl. Beat at low speed of electric mixer until smooth. Spread over base. Refrigerate 30 minutes.

**7. For Chocolate Glaze,** place chocolate and shortening in small microwave-safe bowl. Microwave at 50% (MEDIUM) for 1 to 2 minutes or until shiny and soft. Stir until smooth. Cool slightly. Spread over peanut butter layer. Refrigerate about 1 hour or until glaze is set. Cut into 3×1½-inch bars. Let stand 15 to 20 minutes at room temperature before serving.

*Makes about 2 dozen bars*

*Triple Layer Peanut Butter Bars*

# — *Time-Honored* —

# BROWNIES

### DECADENT BLONDE BROWNIES

½ cup butter or margarine, softened
¾ cup granulated sugar
¾ cup firmly packed light brown sugar
2 large eggs
2 teaspoons vanilla
1½ cups all-purpose flour
1 teaspoon baking powder
½ teaspoon salt
1 package (10 ounces) semisweet chocolate chunks
1 jar (3½ ounces) macadamia nuts, coarsely chopped

Preheat oven to 350°F. Beat butter, granulated sugar and brown sugar in large bowl with electric mixer at medium speed until light and fluffy. Beat in eggs and vanilla. Add combined flour, baking powder and salt. Stir until well blended. Stir in chocolate chunks and macadamia nuts. Spread evenly into greased 13×9-inch baking pan. Bake 25 to 30 minutes or until golden brown. Remove pan to wire rack; cool completely. Cut into 3¼×1½-inch bars.      *Makes about 2 dozen brownies*

## BROWNIES

## RASPBERRY FUDGE BROWNIES

½ **cup butter or margarine**
3 **squares (1 ounce each) bittersweet chocolate***
2 **eggs**
1 **cup sugar**
1 **teaspoon vanilla**
¾ **cup all-purpose flour**
¼ **teaspoon baking powder**
   **Dash salt**
½ **cup sliced or slivered almonds**
½ **cup raspberry preserves**
1 **cup (6 ounces) milk chocolate chips**

*Bittersweet chocolate is available in specialty food stores. One square unsweetened chocolate plus 2 squares semisweet chocolate may be substituted.

Preheat oven to 350°F. Butter and flour 8-inch square baking pan. Melt butter and bittersweet chocolate in small, heavy saucepan over low heat. Remove from heat; cool. Beat eggs, sugar and vanilla in large bowl until light. Beat in chocolate mixture. Stir in flour, baking powder and salt until just blended. Spread ¾ of batter in prepared pan; sprinkle almonds over top. Bake 10 minutes. Remove from oven; spread preserves over almonds. Carefully spoon remaining batter over preserves, smoothing top. Bake 25 to 30 minutes or just until top feels firm. Remove from oven; sprinkle chocolate chips over top. Let stand a few minutes, then spread evenly over brownies. Cool completely. When chocolate is set, cut into squares.

*Makes 16 brownies*

## WHITE CHOCOLATE CHUNK BROWNIES

4 **squares (1 ounce each) unsweetened chocolate, coarsely chopped**
½ **cup butter or margarine**
2 **large eggs**
1¼ **cups granulated sugar**
1 **teaspoon vanilla**
½ **cup all-purpose flour**
½ **teaspoon salt**
1 **white baking bar (6 ounces), cut into ¼-inch pieces**
½ **cup coarsely chopped walnuts (optional)**
   **Powdered sugar for garnish**

Preheat oven to 350°F. Melt unsweetened chocolate and butter in small, heavy saucepan over low heat, stirring constantly; set aside. Beat eggs in large bowl; gradually add granulated sugar, beating at medium speed about 4 minutes until very thick and lemon colored. Beat in chocolate mixture and vanilla. Beat in flour and salt just until blended. Stir in baking bar pieces and walnuts. Spread evenly into greased 8-inch square baking pan. Bake 30 minutes or until edges begin to pull away from sides of pan and center is set. Remove pan to wire rack; cool completely. Cut into 2-inch squares. Sprinkle with powdered sugar, if desired.

*Makes about 16 brownies*

*Raspberry Fudge Brownies*

## BROWNIES

## TOFFEE BROWNIE BARS

**CRUST**
- ¾ **cup butter or margarine, softened**
- ¾ **cup firmly packed brown sugar**
- 1 **egg yolk**
- ¾ **teaspoon vanilla extract**
- 1½ **cups all-purpose flour**

**FILLING**
- 1 **package (19.8 ounces) DUNCAN HINES®**
  **Fudge Brownie Mix**
- 1 **egg**
- ⅓ **cup water**
- ⅓ **cup CRISCO® Oil**

**TOPPING**
- 1 **package (12 ounces) milk chocolate**
  **chips, melted**
- ¾ **cup finely chopped pecans**

**1.** Preheat oven to 350°F. Grease 15½×10½×1-inch jelly-roll pan.

**2. For Crust,** combine butter, brown sugar, egg yolk and vanilla extract in large bowl. Stir in flour. Spread in pan. Bake 15 minutes or until golden.

**3. For Filling,** combine brownie mix, egg, water and oil in large bowl. Stir with spoon until well blended, about 50 strokes. Spread over hot crust. Bake 15 minutes or until surface appears set. Cool 30 minutes.

**4. For Topping,** spread melted chocolate on top of brownie layer; garnish with pecans. Cool completely in pan on wire rack. Cut into bars.

*Makes about 48 brownies*

## EXTRA MOIST & CHUNKY BROWNIES

- 1 **(8-ounce) package cream cheese,**
  **softened**
- 1 **cup sugar**
- 1 **egg**
- 1 **teaspoon vanilla extract**
- ¾ **cup all-purpose flour**
- 1 **(4-serving size) package ROYAL®**
  **Chocolate or Dark 'n' Sweet Chocolate**
  **Pudding & Pie Filling**
- 4 **(1-ounce) semisweet chocolate squares,**
  **chopped**

**MICROWAVE DIRECTIONS:** In large bowl, with electric mixer at high speed, beat cream cheese, sugar, egg and vanilla until smooth; blend in flour and pudding mix. Spread batter in greased 8×8×2-inch microwavable dish; sprinkle with chocolate. Microwave on HIGH (100% power) for 8 to 10 minutes or until toothpick inserted in center comes out clean, rotating dish ½ turn every 2 minutes. Cool completely in pan. Cut into squares.

*Makes 16 squares*

*Toffee Brownie Bars*

# BROWNIES

## CARAMEL-LAYERED BROWNIES

    4 squares BAKER'S® Unsweetened
        Chocolate
  ¾ cup (1½ sticks) margarine or butter
    2 cups sugar
    3 eggs
    1 teaspoon vanilla
    1 cup all-purpose flour
    1 cup BAKER'S® Semi-Sweet Real
        Chocolate Chips
 1½ cups chopped nuts
    1 package (14 ounces) caramels
  ⅓ cup evaporated milk

HEAT oven to 350°F.

MICROWAVE chocolate and margarine in large microwavable bowl on HIGH 2 minutes or until margarine is melted. **Stir until chocolate is completely melted.**

STIR sugar into melted chocolate mixture. Mix in eggs and vanilla until well blended. Stir in flour. Remove 1 cup of batter; set aside. Spread remaining batter in greased 13×9-inch pan. Sprinkle with chips and 1 cup of the nuts.

MICROWAVE caramels and milk in same bowl on HIGH 4 minutes, stirring after 2 minutes. Stir until caramels are completely melted and smooth. Spoon over chips and nuts, spreading to edges of pan. Gently spread reserved batter over caramel mixture. Sprinkle with the remaining ½ cup nuts.

BAKE for 40 minutes or until toothpick inserted into center comes out with fudgy crumbs. **Do not overbake.** Cool in pan; cut into squares.

*Makes about 24 brownies*

## BLONDE BRICKLE BROWNIES

 1⅓ cups all-purpose flour
  ½ teaspoon baking powder
  ¼ teaspoon salt
  2 eggs
  ½ cup granulated sugar
  ½ cup firmly packed brown sugar
  ⅓ cup butter or margarine, melted
  1 teaspoon vanilla
  ¼ teaspoon almond extract
  1 package (6 ounces) BITS 'O BRICKLE®,
    divided
  ½ cup chopped pecans (optional)

Preheat oven to 350°F. Grease 8-inch square baking pan. Mix flour with baking powder and salt; set aside. In large bowl, beat eggs well. Gradually beat in granulated sugar and brown sugar until thick and creamy. Add butter, vanilla and almond extract; mix well. Gently stir in flour mixture until moistened. Fold in ⅔ cup Bits 'O Brickle® and nuts. Pour into prepared pan.

Bake 30 minutes. Remove from oven; immediately sprinkle remaining Bits 'O Brickle® over top. Cool completely in pan on wire rack. Cut into squares.

*Makes about 16 brownies*

*Blonde Brickle Brownies*

# BROWNIES

## SCRUMPTIOUS MINTED BROWNIES

**1 package (19.8 ounces) DUNCAN HINES®**
**Fudge Brownie Mix**
**1 egg**
**⅓ cup water**
**⅓ cup CRISCO® Oil**
**48 chocolate crème de menthe candy wafers,**
**divided**

**1.** Preheat oven to 350°F. Grease bottom of
13×9×2-inch baking pan.

**2.** Combine brownie mix, egg, water and oil in
large bowl. Stir with spoon until well blended,
about 50 strokes. Spread in pan. Bake at 350°F for
25 minutes or until set. Place 30 candy wafers
evenly over hot brownies. Let stand for 1 minute
to melt. Spread candy wafers to frost brownies.
Score frosting into 36 bars by running tip of knife
through melted candy. (Do not cut through
brownies.) Cut remaining 18 candy wafers in half
lengthwise; place halves on each scored bar. Cool
completely. Cut into bars.　　*Makes 36 brownies*

**TIP:** For a unique garnish, in place of candy wafer
halves, make chocolate mint wafer curls. Pull a
vegetable peeler firmly across sides of candy
wafers. Use long, thin strokes. Arrange on top of
brownies while frosting is still soft.

## BUFFALO BILL BROWNIES

**1 (4-serving size) package ROYAL®**
**Chocolate Pudding & Pie Filling**
**2 cups heavy cream**
**¼ cup raspberry preserves**
**1 prepared brownie mix in 9-inch square**
**pan**
**¼ cup semisweet chocolate chips**
**1 tablespoon FLEISCHMANN'S® Margarine**

In small saucepan, over medium heat, heat
pudding, heavy cream and preserves to a boil; boil
1 minute. Pour pudding over prepared brownie; set
aside.

In small saucepan, over medium heat, melt
chocolate chips and margarine. Drizzle over
pudding. Chill until firm, about 2 hours. Cut into
3-inch squares.　　*Makes 9 servings*

*Scrumptious Minted Brownies*

**BROWNIES**

## BROWNIE BON BONS

**2 jars (10 ounces each) maraschino
cherries with stems
Cherry liqueur (optional)\***
**4 squares BAKER'S® Unsweetened
Chocolate**
**¾ cup (1½ sticks) margarine or butter**
**2 cups granulated sugar**
**4 eggs**
**1 teaspoon vanilla**
**1 cup all-purpose flour**
**Chocolate Fudge Filling (recipe follows)**
**½ cup powdered sugar**

\*For liqueur-flavored cherries, drain liquid from cherries. Do not remove cherries from jars. Refill jars with liqueur to completely cover cherries; cover tightly. Let stand at least 24 hours for best flavor.

HEAT oven to 350°F.

MICROWAVE chocolate and margarine in large microwavable bowl on HIGH 2 minutes or until margarine is melted. **Stir until chocolate is completely melted.**

STIR granulated sugar into melted chocolate mixture. Mix in eggs and vanilla until well blended. Stir in flour. Fill greased 1¾×1-inch miniature muffin cups ⅔ full with batter.

BAKE for 20 minutes or until toothpick inserted into center comes out with fudgy crumbs. **Do not overbake.** Cool slightly; loosen edges with tip of knife. Remove from pans. Turn each brownie onto wax paper-lined tray while warm. Make ½-inch indentation into top of each brownie with end of wooden spoon. Cool completely.

PREPARE Chocolate Fudge Filling. Drain cherries, reserving liquid or liqueur. Let cherries stand on paper towels to dry. Combine powdered sugar with enough reserved liquid to form a thin glaze.

SPOON or pipe about 1 teaspoon Chocolate Fudge Filling into indentation of each brownie. Gently press cherry into filling. Drizzle with powdered sugar glaze.    *Makes about 48 bon bons*

**CHOCOLATE FUDGE FILLING**
**1 package (3 ounces) PHILADELPHIA
BRAND® Cream Cheese, softened**
**1 teaspoon vanilla**
**¼ cup corn syrup**
**3 squares BAKER'S® Unsweetened
Chocolate, melted and cooled**
**1 cup powdered sugar**

BEAT cream cheese and vanilla in small bowl until smooth. Slowly pour in corn syrup, beating until well blended. Add chocolate; beat until smooth. Gradually add powdered sugar, beating until well blended and smooth.

*Makes about 1 cup*

*Brownie Bon Bons*

BROWNIES

## COCONUT CROWNED CAPPUCCINO BROWNIES

**6 squares (1 ounce each) semisweet**
    **chocolate, coarsely chopped**
**1 tablespoon freeze-dried coffee**
**1 tablespoon boiling water**
**¾ cup all-purpose flour**
**¾ teaspoon ground cinnamon**
**½ teaspoon baking powder**
**¼ teaspoon salt**
**½ cup sugar**
**¼ cup butter or margarine, softened**
**3 large eggs, divided**
**¼ cup whipping cream**
**1 teaspoon vanilla**
**¾ cup flaked coconut, divided**
**½ cup semisweet chocolate chips, divided**

**1.** Preheat oven to 350°F. Grease 8-inch square baking pan; set aside.

**2.** Melt chocolate squares in small, heavy saucepan over low heat, stirring constantly; set aside. Dissolve coffee in boiling water in small cup; set aside.

**3.** In small bowl, combine flour, cinnamon, baking powder and salt.

**4.** Beat sugar and butter in large bowl with electric mixer at medium speed until light and fluffy. Beat in 2 eggs, 1 at a time, scraping down side of bowl after each addition. Beat in chocolate mixture and coffee mixture until well combined. Add flour mixture. Beat at low speed until well blended. Spread batter evenly into prepared pan.

**5.** For topping, combine cream, remaining 1 egg and vanilla in small bowl; mix well. Stir in ½ cup coconut and ¼ cup chips. Spread evenly over brownie base; sprinkle with remaining ¼ cup coconut and chips.

**6.** Bake 30 to 35 minutes or until coconut is browned and center is set. Remove pan to wire rack; cool completely. Cut into 2-inch squares. Store tightly covered at room temperature or freeze up to 3 months. *Makes 16 brownies*

*Coconut Crowned Cappuccino Brownies*

BROWNIES

# CHOCOLATEY ROCKY ROAD BROWNIES

## BROWNIES
   1 cup butter or margarine
   4 squares (1 ounce each) unsweetened
      chocolate
1½ cups granulated sugar
   1 cup all-purpose flour
   3 eggs
1½ teaspoons vanilla
   ½ cup salted peanuts, chopped

## FROSTING
   ¼ cup butter or margarine
   1 (3-ounce) package cream cheese
   1 square (1 ounce) unsweetened chocolate
   ¼ cup milk
2¾ cups powdered sugar
   1 teaspoon vanilla
   2 cups miniature marshmallows
   1 cup salted peanuts

**For Brownies,** preheat oven to 350°F. In 3-quart saucepan, combine 1 cup butter and 4 squares chocolate. Cook over medium heat, stirring constantly, until melted, 5 to 7 minutes. Add granulated sugar, flour, eggs and 1½ teaspoons vanilla; mix well. Stir in ½ cup chopped peanuts. Spread into greased 13×9-inch baking pan. Bake 20 to 25 minutes or until brownie starts to pull away from sides of pan. Cool completely.

**For Frosting,** in 2-quart saucepan, combine ¼ cup butter, cream cheese, 1 square chocolate and milk. Cook over medium heat, stirring occasionally, until melted, 6 to 8 minutes. Remove from heat; add powdered sugar and 1 teaspoon vanilla; beat with hand mixer until smooth. Stir in marshmallows and 1 cup peanuts. Immediately spread over cooled brownies. Cool completely; cut into bars. Store in refrigerator.    *Makes about 4 dozen brownies*

*Chocolatey Rocky Road Brownies*

# — *Grandkids'* —

# DELIGHTS

## CHOCOLATE CHIP LOLLIPOPS

**1 package DUNCAN HINES® Chocolate Chip Cookie Mix**
**1 egg**
**⅓ cup CRISCO® Oil**
**2 tablespoons water**
**Flat ice cream sticks**
**Assorted decors**

**1.** Preheat oven to 375°F.

**2.** Combine cookie mix, egg, oil and water in large bowl. Stir until thoroughly blended. Shape dough into 32 (1-inch) balls. Place balls 3 inches apart on ungreased cookie sheets. Push ice cream stick into center of each ball. Flatten dough ball with hand to form round lollipop. Decorate by pressing decors onto dough. Bake at 375°F for 8 to 9 minutes or until light golden brown. Cool 1 minute on cookie sheets. Remove to wire racks. Cool completely. Store in airtight container.

*Makes 2½ to 3 dozen cookies*

**DELIGHTS**

## PEANUT BUTTER BEARS

**1 cup SKIPPY® Creamy Peanut Butter**
**1 cup MAZOLA® Margarine, softened**
**1 cup firmly packed brown sugar**
**⅔ cup KARO® Light or Dark Corn Syrup**
**2 eggs**
**4 cups all-purpose flour, divided**
**1 tablespoon baking powder**
**1 teaspoon ground cinnamon (optional)**
**¼ teaspoon salt**

In large bowl, with mixer at medium speed, beat peanut butter, margarine, brown sugar, corn syrup and eggs until smooth. Reduce speed; beat in 2 cups of the flour, the baking powder, cinnamon and salt. With spoon, stir in remaining 2 cups flour. Wrap dough in plastic wrap; refrigerate 2 hours.

Preheat oven to 325°F. Divide dough in half; set aside half. On floured surface, roll out half the dough to ⅛-inch thickness. Cut with floured bear cookie cutter. Repeat with remaining dough. Bake on ungreased cookie sheets 10 minutes or until lightly browned. Remove from cookie sheets; cool completely on wire rack. Decorate as desired.

*Makes about 3 dozen bears*

**Prep Time:** 35 minutes, plus chilling
**Bake Time:** 10 minutes, plus cooling

**NOTE:** Use scraps of dough to make bear faces. Make one small ball of dough for muzzle. Form 3 smaller balls of dough and press gently to create eyes and nose; bake as directed. If desired, use frosting to create paws, ears and bow ties.

## MARSHMALLOW KRISPIE BARS

**1 package (19.8 ounces) DUNCAN HINES® Fudge Brownie Mix**
**1 package (10½ ounces) miniature marshmallows**
**1½ cups semi-sweet chocolate chips**
**1 cup JIF® Creamy Peanut Butter**
**1 tablespoon butter or margarine**
**1½ cups crisp rice cereal**

**1.** Preheat oven to 350°F. Grease bottom of 13×9×2-inch baking pan.

**2.** Prepare and bake brownies following package directions for original recipe. Remove from oven. Sprinkle marshmallows on hot brownies. Return to oven. Bake for 3 minutes longer.

**3.** Place chocolate chips, peanut butter and butter in medium saucepan. Cook on low heat, stirring constantly, until chips are melted. Add rice cereal; mix well. Spread mixture over marshmallow layer. Refrigerate until chilled. Cut into bars.

*Makes 24 bars*

*Peanut Butter Bears*

DELIGHTS

## PEANUT BUTTER PIZZA COOKIES

    1 package DUNCAN HINES® Peanut Butter Cookie Mix
    1 egg
    ¼ cup CRISCO® Oil
    1 tablespoon water
    Sugar
    1 container (16 ounces) DUNCAN HINES® Creamy Homestyle Chocolate Frosting
    Cashews
    Candy-coated chocolate pieces
    Gumdrops, halved
    Flaked coconut
    ½ bar (2 ounces) white chocolate baking bar
    1½ teaspoons CRISCO® All-Vegetable Shortening

**1.** Preheat oven to 375°F.

**2.** Combine cookie mix, peanut butter packet from Mix, egg, oil and water in large bowl. Stir until thoroughly blended. Shape into 12 (2-inch) balls (about 3 level tablespoons each). Place balls 3½ inches apart on ungreased cookie sheets. Flatten with bottom of large glass dipped in sugar to make 3-inch circles. Bake at 375°F for 9 to 11 minutes or until set. Cool 1 minute on cookie sheets. Remove to wire racks. Cool completely.

**3.** Frost cookies with Chocolate frosting. Decorate with cashews, candy pieces, gumdrops and coconut. Melt white chocolate and shortening in small saucepan on low heat, stirring constantly, until smooth. Drizzle over cookies.

*Makes 12 large cookies*

## CRUMBLE BARS

    ½ cup butter or margarine
    1 cup all-purpose flour
    ¾ cup quick-cooking oats, uncooked
    ⅓ cup firmly packed light brown sugar
    ½ teaspoon salt
    ½ teaspoon baking soda
    ½ teaspoon vanilla extract
    4 MILKY WAY® Bars (2.15 ounces each), each cut into 8 slices

Preheat oven to 350°F. Lightly grease 8×8×2-inch baking pan; set aside.

Melt butter in large saucepan. Remove from heat; stir in flour, oats, sugar, salt, baking soda and vanilla. Blend until crumbly. Press ⅔ of mixture into prepared pan. Arrange MILKY WAY® Bar slices in pan to within ½ inch from edges. Finely crumble remaining mixture over the MILKY WAY® Bars. Bake 20 to 25 minutes or until edges are golden brown. Cool in pan on wire rack. Cut into bars or squares to serve.

*Makes 12 to 16 bars*

*Peanut Butter Pizza Cookies*

DELIGHTS

## WATERMELON SLICES

- 1 package DUNCAN HINES® Golden Sugar
  Cookie Mix
- 1 egg
- ¼ cup CRISCO® Oil
- 1½ tablespoons water
- 12 drops red food coloring
- 5 drops green food coloring
- Chocolate sprinkles

**1.** Combine cookie mix, egg, oil and water in large bowl. Stir until thoroughly blended; reserve ⅓ cup dough.

**2.** For red cookie dough, combine remaining dough with red food coloring. Stir until evenly tinted. On waxed paper, shape dough into 12-inch-long roll with one side flattened. Cover; refrigerate with flat side down until firm.

**3.** For green cookie dough, combine reserved ⅓ cup dough with green food coloring in small bowl. Stir until evenly tinted. Place between 2 layers of waxed paper. Roll dough into 12×4-inch rectangle. Refrigerate for 15 minutes.

**4.** Preheat oven to 375°F.

**5.** To assemble, remove green dough rectangle from refrigerator. Remove top layer of waxed paper. Trim edges along both 12-inch sides. Remove red dough log from refrigerator. Place red dough log, flattened side up, along center of green dough. Mold green dough up to edge of flattened side of red dough. Remove bottom layer of waxed paper. Trim excess green dough, if necessary.

**6.** Cut chilled roll with flat side down into ¼-inch-thick slices with sharp knife. Place 2 inches apart on ungreased cookie sheets. Sprinkle chocolate sprinkles on red dough for seeds. Bake at 375°F for 7 minutes or until set. Cool 1 minute on cookie sheets. Remove to wire racks. Cool completely. Store between layers of waxed paper in airtight container.     *Makes 3 to 4 dozen cookies*

**TIP:** To make neat, clean slices, use unwaxed dental floss.

*Watermelon Slices*

DELIGHTS

## CHOCOLATEY PEANUT BUTTER GOODIES

**COOKIES**
  1 CRISCO® Stick or 1 cup CRISCO®
    All-Vegetable Shortening
  4 cups (1 pound) powdered sugar
  1½ cups JIF® Extra Crunchy Peanut Butter
  1½ cups graham cracker crumbs

**FROSTING**
  1 tablespoon CRISCO® All-Vegetable
    Shortening
  1⅓ cups semi-sweet chocolate chips

**1. For Cookies,** combine shortening, powdered sugar, peanut butter and crumbs in large bowl with spoon. Spread evenly on bottom of 13×9-inch baking pan.

**2. For Frosting,** combine shortening and chocolate chips in small microwave-safe bowl. Microwave at 50% (MEDIUM). Stir after 1 minute. Repeat until smooth (or melt on rangetop in small saucepan on very low heat). Spread over top of cookie mixture. Cool at least 1 hour or until chocolate hardens. Cut into 2×1½-inch bars.

*Makes 3 dozen bars*

## P. B. GRAHAM SNACKERS

  ½ CRISCO® Stick or ½ cup CRISCO®
    All-Vegetable Shortening
  2 cups powdered sugar
  ¾ cup JIF® Creamy Peanut Butter
  1 cup graham cracker crumbs
  ½ cup semi-sweet chocolate chips
  ½ cup graham cracker crumbs, crushed
    peanuts or chocolate sprinkles
    (optional)

**1.** Combine shortening, powdered sugar and peanut butter in large bowl. Beat at low speed of electric mixer until well blended. Stir in 1 cup crumbs and chocolate chips. Cover and refrigerate 1 hour.

**2.** Form dough into 1-inch balls. Roll in ½ cup crumbs, peanuts or sprinkles for a fancier cookie. Cover and refrigerate until ready to serve.

*Makes about 3 dozen cookies*

*Top to bottom: P.B. Graham Snackers and Chocolatey Peanut Butter Goodies*

# DELIGHTS

## KIDS' FAVORITE JUMBO CHIPPERS

2¼ cups all-purpose flour
1 teaspoon baking soda
¾ teaspoon salt
1 cup butter or margarine, softened
¾ cup granulated sugar
¾ cup firmly packed brown sugar
2 large eggs
1 teaspoon vanilla
1 package (12 ounces) mini baking semi-sweet chocolate candies
1 cup peanut butter flavored chips

**1.** Preheat oven to 375°F.

**2.** Combine flour, baking soda and salt in medium bowl.

**3.** Beat butter, granulated sugar and brown sugar in large bowl with electric mixer at medium speed until light and fluffy. Beat in eggs and vanilla. Add flour mixture. Beat at low speed until well blended. Stir in candies and chips.

**4.** Drop heaping tablespoonfuls of dough 3 inches apart onto *ungreased* cookie sheets.

**5.** Bake 10 to 12 minutes or until edges are golden brown. Let cookies stand on cookie sheets 2 minutes. Remove cookies with spatula to wire racks; cool completely. Store tightly covered at room temperature or freeze up to 3 months.

*Makes 3 dozen jumbo cookies*

## CAP'N'S COOKIES

1 cup firmly packed brown sugar
½ cup (1 stick) margarine or butter, softened
2 eggs
1 teaspoon vanilla
1½ cups all-purpose flour
1 teaspoon baking powder
½ teaspoon salt (optional)
2 cups CAP'N CRUNCH® Cereal, any flavor, coarsely crushed
1 cup raisins or semi-sweet chocolate pieces

Preheat oven to 375°F. Lightly grease cookie sheet. Beat sugar and margarine until fluffy. Blend in eggs and vanilla. Add combined flour, baking powder and salt; mix well. Stir in cereal and raisins. Drop by rounded teaspoonfuls onto prepared cookie sheet. Bake 10 to 12 minutes or until light golden brown. Cool 2 minutes on cookie sheet; remove to wire rack. Cool completely. Store tightly covered.

*Makes about 3 dozen cookies*

*Kids' Favorite Jumbo Chippers*

# — Old-World —
# HOLIDAY TREATS

### GOLDEN KOLACKY

**¼ cup butter, softened**
**4 ounces cream cheese, softened**
**1 cup all-purpose flour**
**Fruit preserves**

Combine butter and cream cheese in large bowl; beat until smooth. Gradually add flour to butter mixture, blending until soft dough forms. Divide dough in half; wrap each half in plastic wrap. Refrigerate until firm.

Preheat oven to 375°F. Roll out dough, ½ at a time, on floured surface to ⅛-inch thickness. Cut into 3-inch squares. Spoon 1 teaspoon preserves in center of each square. Bring up two opposite corners to center; pinch together tightly to seal. Fold sealed tip to one side; pinch to seal. Place 1 inch apart on ungreased cookie sheets. Bake for 10 to 15 minutes or until lightly browned. Remove to cooling racks; cool completely.

*Makes about 2½ dozen cookies*

## PEANUT BUTTER REINDEER

**COOKIES:**
    **1 package DUNCAN HINES® Peanut Butter
        Cookie Mix**
    **1 egg**
    **¼ cup CRISCO® Oil**
    **4 teaspoons all-purpose flour, divided**

**ASSORTED DECORATIONS:**
    **Miniature semi-sweet chocolate chips**
    **Vanilla milk chips**
    **Candy-coated semi-sweet chocolate chips**
    **Colored sprinkles**

**1. For Cookies,** combine cookie mix, peanut butter packet from Mix, egg and oil in large bowl. Stir until thoroughly blended. Form dough into ball; divide in half to make 2 balls. Place 2 teaspoons of flour in gallon size (10⁹/₁₆×11-inch) resealable plastic bag. Place one ball of dough in bag. Seal bag; shake to coat with flour. Place dough in center of bag; unseal. Roll dough with rolling pin out to edges of bag. Slide bag onto baking sheet. Repeat with remaining 2 teaspoons flour, second plastic bag and remaining dough ball. Chill in refrigerator at least 1 hour.

**2.** Preheat oven to 375°F.

**3.** Use scissors to cut one bag down center and across ends. Turn plastic back to uncover dough. Dip reindeer cookie cutter in flour. Cut dough with reindeer cookie cutter. Dip cookie cutter in flour after each cut. Transfer cutout cookie to ungreased cookie sheets using a pancake turner. Decorate as desired making eyes, mouth, nose and tail with assorted decorations. Bake at 375°F for 5 to 7 minutes or until set but not browned. Cool 2 minutes on cookie sheet. Remove to wire racks. Cool completely. Repeat with remaining chilled dough. Store cookies between layers of waxed paper in airtight container.

*Makes about 2 dozen cookies*

**TIPS:** Reroll dough by folding plastic back over dough. To use as ornaments, press end of drinking straw in top of each unbaked cookie to make hole. Press straw through cookie again after baking. String ribbon through holes of cooled cookies. Tie at top.

*Peanut Butter Reindeer*

## WALNUT CHRISTMAS BALLS

**1 cup California walnuts**
**⅔ cup powdered sugar, divided**
**1 cup butter or margarine, softened**
**1 teaspoon vanilla**
**1¾ cups all-purpose flour**
**Chocolate Filling (recipe follows)**

Preheat oven to 350°F. In food processor or blender, process walnuts with 2 tablespoons sugar until finely ground. In large bowl, cream butter and remaining sugar. Beat in vanilla. Add flour and ¾ cup walnut mixture; beat until blended. Roll dough into about 3 dozen walnut-size balls. Place 2 inches apart on ungreased cookie sheets.

Bake 10 to 12 minutes or until just golden around edges. Remove to wire racks to cool completely. Prepare Chocolate Filling. Place generous teaspoonful of filling on flat side of half the cookies. Top with remaining cookies, flat side down, forming sandwiches. Roll chocolate edges of cookies in remaining ground walnuts.

*Makes about 1½ dozen sandwich cookies*

**CHOCOLATE FILLING:** Chop 3 squares (1 ounce each) semisweet chocolate into small pieces; place in food processor or blender with ½ teaspoon vanilla. In small saucepan, heat 2 tablespoons *each* butter or margarine and whipping cream over medium heat until hot; pour over chocolate. Process until chocolate is melted, turning machine off and scraping sides as needed. With machine running, gradually add 1 cup powdered sugar; process until smooth.

*Favorite recipe from* **Walnut Marketing Board**

## BANANA CRESCENTS

**½ cup DOLE® Chopped Almonds, toasted**
**6 tablespoons sugar, divided**
**½ cup margarine, cut into pieces**
**1½ cups plus 2 tablespoons all-purpose flour**
**⅛ teaspoon salt**
**1 extra-ripe, medium DOLE® Banana, peeled**
**2 to 3 ounces semisweet chocolate chips**

Pulverize almonds with 2 tablespoons sugar in food processor.

Beat margarine, almond mixture, remaining 4 tablespoons sugar, flour and salt.

Puree banana; add to batter and mix until well blended.

Using 1 tablespoon batter, roll into log then shape into crescent. Place on ungreased cookie sheet. Bake in 375°F oven 25 minutes or until golden. Cool on wire rack.

Melt chocolate in microwavable dish at 50% power 1½ to 2 minutes, stirring once. Dip ends of cookies in chocolate. Refrigerate until chocolate hardens.

*Makes 2 dozen cookies*

*Banana Crescents*

## GLAZED SUGAR COOKIES

**COOKIES**
　　1 package DUNCAN HINES® Golden Sugar
　　　　Cookie Mix
　　1 egg
　　¼ cup CRISCO® Oil
　　1 teaspoon water

**GLAZE**
　　1½ cups sifted powdered sugar
　　2 to 3 tablespoons water or milk
　　¾ teaspoons vanilla extract
　　　　Food coloring
　　　　Red and green sugar crystals, nonpareils
　　　　or cinnamon candies

**1.** Preheat oven to 375°F.

**2. For Cookies,** combine cookie mix, egg, oil and water in large bowl. Stir thoroughly until blended. Roll dough to ¼-inch thickness on lightly floured surface. Cut dough into desired shapes using floured cookie cutters. Place cookies 2 inches apart on ungreased cookie sheets. Bake at 375°F for 7 to 8 minutes or until edges are light golden brown. Cool 1 minute on cookie sheets. Remove to wire racks. Cool completely.

**3. For Glaze,** combine powdered sugar, water and vanilla extract in medium bowl. Beat until smooth. Tint glaze with food coloring, if desired. Brush glaze on each cookie with a clean pastry brush. Sprinkle each cookie with sugar crystals, nonpareils or cinnamon candies before glaze sets. Allow glaze to set before storing between layers of waxed paper in air-tight container.

*Makes 4 dozen cookies*

**TIP:** Use Duncan Hines Creamy Homestyle Vanilla Frosting for a quick glaze. Heat frosting in opened container in microwave oven at HIGH (100% power) for 10 to 15 seconds. Stir well. Spread on cookies and decorate as desired before frosting sets.

*Glazed Sugar Cookies*

# DANISH RASPBERRY RIBBONS

## COOKIES
    **1 cup butter, softened**
    **½ cup granulated sugar**
    **1 large egg**
    **2 tablespoons milk**
    **2 tablespoons vanilla**
    **¼ teaspoon almond extract**
    **2 to 2⅔ cups all-purpose flour, divided**
    **6 tablespoons seedless raspberry jam**

## GLAZE
    **½ cup sifted powdered sugar**
    **1 tablespoon milk**
    **1 teaspoon vanilla**

**1. For Cookies,** beat butter and granulated sugar in bowl with mixer at medium speed until fluffy. Beat in egg, 2 tablespoons milk, 2 tablespoons vanilla and almond extract until blended.

**2.** Gradually add 1½ cups flour. Beat at low speed until well blended. Stir in additional flour with spoon until stiff dough forms. Wrap in plastic wrap and refrigerate until firm, 30 minutes or overnight.

**3.** Preheat oven to 375°F. Cut dough into 6 pieces. Rewrap 3 pieces; refrigerate. With floured hands, shape each dough piece into 12-inch-long, ¾-inch-thick rope.

**4.** Place ropes 2 inches apart on *ungreased* cookie sheets. Make a ¼-inch-deep groove down center of each rope with handle of wooden spoon. (Ropes flatten to ½-inch-thick strips.)

**5.** Bake 12 minutes. Spoon 1 tablespoon jam along each groove. Bake 5 to 7 minutes longer or until strips are light golden brown. Cool strips 15 minutes on cookie sheets.

**6. For Glaze,** place powdered sugar, 1 tablespoon milk and 1 teaspoon vanilla in small bowl; stir until smooth. Drizzle Glaze over strips; let stand 5 minutes to dry. Cut strips at 45° angle into 1-inch slices. Cool cookies completely on wire racks. Repeat with remaining dough. Store tightly covered between sheets of waxed paper at room temperature. *Makes about 5½ dozen cookies*

*Danish Raspberry Ribbons*

HOLIDAY TREATS

## PEANUT BUTTER CUT-OUTS

½ cup **SKIPPY**® Creamy Peanut Butter
6 tablespoons **MAZOLA**® Margarine or
butter, softened
½ cup firmly packed brown sugar
⅓ cup **KARO**® Light or Dark Corn Syrup
1 egg
2 cups all-purpose flour, divided
1½ teaspoons baking powder
1 teaspoon ground cinnamon (optional)
⅛ teaspoon salt

In large bowl, with mixer at medium speed, beat peanut butter, margarine, brown sugar, corn syrup and egg until smooth. Reduce speed; beat in 1 cup flour, baking powder, cinnamon and salt. With spoon, stir in remaining 1 cup flour.

Divide dough in half. Between two sheets of waxed paper on large cookie sheets, roll each half of dough to ¼-inch thickness. Refrigerate until firm, about 1 hour.

Preheat oven to 350°F. Remove top piece of waxed paper. With floured cookie cutters, cut dough into shapes. Place on ungreased cookie sheets. Bake 10 minutes or until lightly browned. *Do not overbake.* Let stand on cookie sheets 2 minutes. Remove from cookie sheets; cool completely on wire racks. Reroll dough trimmings and cut. Decorate as desired. *Makes about 5 dozen cookies*

**NOTE:** Use scraps of dough to create details on cookies.

## BAVARIAN COOKIE WREATHS

3½ cups unsifted all-purpose flour
1 cup sugar, divided
3 teaspoons grated orange peel, divided
¼ teaspoon salt
1⅓ cups butter or margarine
¼ cup Florida orange juice
⅓ cup finely chopped blanched almonds
1 egg white beaten with 1 teaspoon water
Prepared frosting (optional)

Preheat oven to 400°F. In large bowl, mix flour, ¾ cup sugar, 2 teaspoons orange peel and salt. Using pastry blender, cut in butter and orange juice until mixture holds together. Knead few times and press into a ball.

Shape dough into ¾-inch balls; lightly roll each ball on floured board into a 6-inch-long strip. Using two strips, twist together to make a rope. Pinch ends of rope together to make a wreath; place on lightly greased baking sheet.

In shallow dish, mix almonds, remaining ¼ cup sugar and 1 teaspoon orange peel. Brush top of each wreath with egg white mixture and sprinkle with sugar-almond mixture.

Bake 8 to 10 minutes or until lightly browned. Remove to wire racks; cool completely. Frost, if desired. *Makes 5 dozen cookies*

*Favorite recipe from **Florida Department of Citrus***

*Peanut Butter Cut-Outs*

# PECAN DATE BARS

**CRUST**
**⅓ cup butter or margarine**
**1 package DUNCAN HINES® Moist Deluxe White Cake Mix**
**1 egg**

**TOPPING**
**1 (8-ounce) package chopped dates**
**1¼ cups chopped pecans**
**1 cup water**
**½ teaspoon vanilla extract**
**Powdered sugar**

**1.** Preheat oven to 350°F. Grease and flour 13×9-inch pan.

**2. For Crust,** cut butter into cake mix with a pastry blender or 2 knives until mixture is crumbly. Add egg; stir well (mixture will be crumbly). Press mixture into bottom of prepared pan.

**3. For Topping,** combine dates, pecans and water in medium saucepan. Bring to a boil. Reduce heat and simmer until mixture thickens, stirring constantly. Remove from heat. Stir in vanilla extract. Spread date mixture evenly over crust. Bake 25 to 30 minutes. Cool completely. Dust with powdered sugar.          *Makes about 32 bars*

# BLACK RUSSIAN BROWNIES

**4 squares (1 ounce each) unsweetened chocolate**
**1 cup butter**
**¾ teaspoon black pepper**
**4 eggs, lightly beaten**
**1½ cups sugar**
**1½ teaspoons vanilla**
**⅓ cup KAHLÚA®**
**2 tablespoons vodka**
**1⅓ cups all-purpose flour**
**½ teaspoon salt**
**¼ teaspoon baking powder**
**1 cup chopped walnuts or toasted sliced almonds**
**Powdered sugar (optional)**

Line bottom of 13×9-inch baking pan with waxed paper. Melt chocolate and butter with pepper in small saucepan over low heat. Remove from heat.

Combine eggs, sugar and vanilla in large bowl; beat well. Stir in cooled chocolate mixture, Kahlúa and vodka. Combine flour, salt and baking powder; add to chocolate mixture and stir until blended. Add walnuts. Spread in prepared pan.

Bake in 350°F oven just until toothpick inserted into center comes out clean, about 25 minutes. *Do not overbake.* Cool in pan on wire rack. Cut into bars. Sprinkle with powdered sugar, if desired.
          *Makes about 30 brownies*

*Pecan Date Bars*

## GERMAN HONEY BARS

2¾ **cups all-purpose flour**
  2 **teaspoons ground cinnamon**
  1 **teaspoon baking powder**
  ½ **teaspoon baking soda**
  ½ **teaspoon salt**
  ½ **teaspoon ground cardamom**
  ½ **teaspoon ground ginger**
  ½ **cup honey**
  ½ **cup dark molasses**
  ¾ **cup firmly packed brown sugar**
  3 **tablespoons butter, melted**
  1 **large egg**
  ½ **cup chopped toasted almonds (optional)**
    **Glaze (recipe follows)**

**1.** Preheat oven to 350°F. Grease 15×10-inch jelly-roll pan; set aside.

**2.** Combine flour, cinnamon, baking powder, baking soda, salt, cardamom and ginger in medium bowl.

**3.** Combine honey and molasses in medium saucepan; bring to a boil over medium heat. Remove from heat; cool 10 minutes.

**4.** Stir brown sugar, butter and egg into honey mixture.

**5.** Place brown sugar mixture in large bowl. Gradually add flour mixture. Beat at low speed with electric mixer until dough forms. Stir in almonds with spoon. (Dough will be slightly sticky.)

**6.** Spread dough evenly into prepared pan. Bake 20 to 22 minutes or until golden brown and set. Remove pan to wire rack; cool completely.

**7.** Prepare Glaze. Spread over cooled cookie base. Let stand until set, about 30 minutes. Cut into 2×1-inch bars. Store tightly covered at room temperature or freeze up to 3 months.

*Makes about 6 dozen bars*

**GLAZE**
  1¼ **cups sifted powdered sugar**
    3 **tablespoons fresh lemon juice**
    1 **teaspoon grated lemon peel**

Place all ingredients in medium bowl; stir with spoon until smooth.

*German Honey Bars*

HOLIDAY TREATS

## CHOCOLATE CHIP RUGALACH

**1 cup (2 sticks) butter or margarine, slightly softened**
**2 cups all-purpose flour**
**1 cup vanilla ice cream, softened**
**½ cup strawberry jam**
**1 cup BAKER'S® Semi-Sweet Real Chocolate Chips**
**1 cup finely chopped nuts**
**Powdered sugar**

**BEAT** butter and flour. Beat in ice cream until well blended. Divide dough into 4 balls; wrap each in waxed paper. Refrigerate until firm, about 1 hour.

**HEAT** oven to 350°F. Roll dough, one ball at a time, on floured surface into 11×6-inch rectangle, about ⅛ inch thick. Spread with 2 tablespoons of the jam; sprinkle with ¼ cup of the chips and ¼ cup of the nuts. Roll up lengthwise as for jelly roll. Place on ungreased cookie sheet. Cut 12 diagonal slits in roll, being careful not to cut all the way through. Repeat with the remaining dough.

**BAKE** for 35 minutes or until golden brown. Cool 5 minutes on cookie sheet. Cut through each roll; separate pieces. Finish cooling on wire racks. Sprinkle with powdered sugar, if desired.

*Makes 4 dozen pieces*

**Prep Time:** 30 minutes
**Chill Time:** 1 hour
**Baking Time:** 35 minutes

## CHOCOLATE ALMOND SHORTBREAD

**¾ cup (1½ sticks) butter or margarine, softened**
**1¼ cups powdered sugar**
**6 squares BAKER'S® Semi-Sweet Chocolate, melted, cooled**
**1 teaspoon vanilla**
**1 cup all-purpose flour**
**¼ teaspoon salt**
**1 cup toasted ground blanched almonds**
**½ cup toasted chopped almonds**

**HEAT** oven to 250°F.

**BEAT** butter and sugar until light and fluffy. Stir in chocolate and vanilla. Mix in flour, salt and ground almonds.

**PRESS** dough into 12×9-inch rectangle on ungreased cookie sheet. Sprinkle with chopped almonds; press lightly into dough.

**BAKE** for 45 to 50 minutes or until set. Cool on cookie sheet; cut into bars.      *Makes about 36 bars*

**Prep Time:** 30 minutes
**Baking Time:** 45 to 50 minutes

*Top to bottom: Chocolate Almond Shortbread, Chocolate Chip Rugalach*

HOLIDAY TREATS

## SUGAR-DUSTED SNOWFLAKES

½ **cup Florida orange juice**
⅓ **cup milk**
1 **tablespoon butter or margarine**
1 **cinnamon stick, 3 inches long**
2 **cups unsifted all-purpose flour**
1½ **teaspoons grated orange peel**
⅛ **teaspoon baking powder**
  **Vegetable oil for frying**
  **Powdered sugar**

In small saucepan, combine orange juice, milk, butter and cinnamon stick. (Mixture will curdle.) Bring to a boil over high heat. Remove from heat; let stand 15 minutes. Remove and discard cinnamon stick.

In large bowl, mix flour, orange peel and baking powder; make well in center. Add warm milk mixture all at once; stir, gradually incorporating flour mixture, until dry ingredients are moistened.

Turn out onto well-floured surface; knead 2 or 3 times until smooth. Cover; let stand 20 minutes to allow dough to cool and become less sticky.

Divide dough in half; roll half on well-floured surface to ⅛-inch thickness. Using floured 3-inch star or round cookie cutter, cut dough into shapes. Place on paper towel and let dry 10 minutes or until tops are dry to the touch. Repeat with remaining dough, rolling scraps together. Cut out small designs in each cookie with canape cutters, so cookie resembles snowflake.

Pour 1 inch of oil in medium skillet; heat to 350°F. Fry cookies, 2 or 3 at a time, turning once until very lightly browned. Drain on paper towels. Cool; sprinkle liberally with powdered sugar.

*Makes 3 dozen cookies*

**COOK'S TIP:** Make sure that the cookies are completely cooled before sprinkling with powdered sugar. If they are still warm, the sugar can melt and become sticky.

*Favorite recipe from* **Florida Department of Citrus**

*Top to bottom: Bavarian Cookie Wreaths (page 112), Sugar-Dusted Snowflakes*

HOLIDAY TREATS

## LINZER SANDWICH COOKIES

**1⅓ cups all-purpose flour**
**¼ teaspoon baking powder**
**¼ teaspoon salt**
**¾ cup sugar**
**½ cup butter, softened**
**1 large egg**
**1 teaspoon vanilla**
**Seedless raspberry jam**

**1.** Combine flour, baking powder and salt in small bowl.

**2.** Beat sugar and butter in medium bowl with electric mixer at medium speed until light and fluffy. Beat in egg and vanilla. Gradually add flour mixture. Beat at low speed until dough forms.

**3.** Form dough into 2 discs; wrap in plastic wrap and refrigerate 2 hours or until firm.

**4.** Preheat oven to 375°F. Working with 1 disc at a time, unwrap dough and place on lightly floured surface. Roll out dough with lightly floured rolling pin.

**5.** Cut dough into desired shapes with floured cookie cutters. Cut out equal numbers of each shape. (If dough becomes soft, cover and refrigerate several minutes before continuing.)

**6.** Cut 1-inch centers out of half the cookies of each shape. Gently press dough trimmings together; reroll and cut out more cookies. Place cookies 1½ to 2 inches apart on *ungreased* cookie sheets.

**7.** Bake 7 to 9 minutes or until edges are lightly browned. Let cookies stand on cookie sheet 1 to 2 minutes. Remove cookies with spatula to wire racks; cool completely. To assemble cookies, spread 1 teaspoon jam on flat side of whole cookies, spreading almost to edges. Place cookies with holes, flat-side down, on jam. Store tightly covered at room temperature or freeze up to 3 months.

*Makes about 2 dozen cookies*

## WALNUT–BRANDY SHORTBREAD

**1 cup butter**
**½ cup firmly packed brown sugar**
**⅛ teaspoon salt**
**2 tablespoons brandy**
**1 cup all-purpose flour**
**1 cup finely chopped toasted California walnuts**
**Granulated sugar**

Cream butter with brown sugar and salt in large bowl; mix in brandy. Gradually add flour; stir in walnuts. Spread in ungreased 9-inch square pan. Refrigerate 30 minutes.

Pierce mixture all over with fork. Bake at 325°F about 55 minutes or until dark golden brown. If dough puffs up during baking, pierce again with fork. Sprinkle lightly with granulated sugar and cool. Cut into squares with sharp knife.

*Makes 36 squares*

*Favorite recipe from* **Walnut Marketing Board**

*Linzer Sandwich Cookies*

# Acknowledgments

**The publishers would like to thank the companies and organizations listed below for the use of their recipes and photos in this publication.**

Best Foods, a Division of CPC International Inc.

California Apricot Advisory Board

Dole Food Company, Inc.

Florida Department of Citrus

Hershey Foods Corporation

Kahlúa Liqueur

Kraft Foods, Inc.

Leaf®, Inc.

M&M/Mars

Nabisco, Inc.

Nestlé Food Company

The Procter & Gamble Company

The Quaker Oats Company

Ralston Foods, Inc.

Sunkist Growers

Walnut Marketing Board

# —Index—

# — *Index* —

# METRIC CONVERSION CHART

## VOLUME MEASUREMENTS (dry)

1/8 teaspoon = 0.5 mL
1/4 teaspoon = 1 mL
1/2 teaspoon = 2 mL
3/4 teaspoon = 4 mL
1 teaspoon = 5 mL
1 tablespoon = 15 mL
2 tablespoons = 30 mL
1/4 cup = 60 mL
1/3 cup = 75 mL
1/2 cup = 125 mL
2/3 cup = 150 mL
3/4 cup = 175 mL
1 cup = 250 mL
2 cups = 1 pint = 500 mL
3 cups = 750 mL
4 cups = 1 quart = 1 L

## VOLUME MEASUREMENTS (fluid)

1 fluid ounce (2 tablespoons) = 30 mL
4 fluid ounces (1/2 cup) = 125 mL
8 fluid ounces (1 cup) = 250 mL
12 fluid ounces (1 1/2 cups) = 375 mL
16 fluid ounces (2 cups) = 500 mL

## WEIGHTS (mass)

1/2 ounce = 15 g
1 ounce = 30 g
3 ounces = 90 g
4 ounces = 120 g
8 ounces = 225 g
10 ounces = 285 g
12 ounces = 360 g
16 ounces = 1 pound = 450 g

## DIMENSIONS

1/16 inch = 2 mm
1/8 inch = 3 mm
1/4 inch = 6 mm
1/2 inch = 1.5 cm
3/4 inch = 2 cm
1 inch = 2.5 cm

## OVEN TEMPERATURES

250°F = 120°C
275°F = 140°C
300°F = 150°C
325°F = 160°C
350°F = 180°C
375°F = 190°C
400°F = 200°C
425°F = 220°C
450°F = 230°C

## BAKING PAN SIZES

| Utensil | Size in Inches/Quarts | Metric Volume | Size in Centimeters |
|---|---|---|---|
| Baking or Cake Pan (square or rectangular) | 8×8×2 | 2 L | 20×20×5 |
| | 9×9×2 | 2.5 L | 22×22×5 |
| | 12×8×2 | 3 L | 30×20×5 |
| | 13×9×2 | 3.5 L | 33×23×5 |
| Loaf Pan | 8×4×3 | 1.5 L | 20×10×7 |
| | 9×5×3 | 2 L | 23×13×7 |
| Round Layer Cake Pan | 8×1½ | 1.2 L | 20×4 |
| | 9×1½ | 1.5 L | 23×4 |
| Pie Plate | 8×1¼ | 750 mL | 20×3 |
| | 9×1¼ | 1 L | 23×3 |
| Baking Dish or Casserole | 1 quart | 1 L | — |
| | 1½ quart | 1.5 L | — |
| | 2 quart | 2 L | — |